There's More to Life!

Craig Selness

While this book is designed for the reader's personal enjoyment, it is also intended for group study. A Leader's Guide with Victor Multiuse Transparency Masters is available from your local bookstore or from the publisher.

VICTOR BOOKS

a division of SP Publications, Inc.
WHEATON, ILLINOIS 60187

Offices also in Fullerton, California • Whitby, Ontario, Canada • Amersham-on-the-Hill, Bucks, England

Unless otherwise noted, Scripture quotations are from the *New American Standard Bible* (NASB), © 1960, 1962, 1968, 1972, 1972, 1973 by The Lockman Foundation, La Habra, California. Other quotations are from *The Holy Bible: Revised Standard Version*, (RSV) © 1952 by the Division of Christian Education of the National Council of the Churches of Christ in the United States; the *New International Version* (NIV), © 1978 by The New York International Bible Society; the *Good News Bible: The Bible in Today's English Version* (GNB), © American Bible Society 1976. Used by permission.

Recommended Dewey Decimal Classification: 248.4
  Suggested Subject Heading: CHRISTIAN LIVING

Library of Congress Catalog Card Number: 81-86287
ISBN: 0-88207-283-8

© 1982 by SP Publications, Inc. All rights reserved
Printed in the United States of America

VICTOR BOOKS
A division of SP Publications, Inc.
P.O. Box 1825 ● Wheaton, Illinois 60187

CONTENTS

1 From Frustration to Fulfillment   **7**

2 When You've Got the Guilties   **15**

3 Alone Again   **29**

4 When Life Loses Its Flavor   **41**

5 The Future Is Now   **54**

6 Who Wants To Kiss a Frog?   **68**

7 When Your Blanket Is in the Wash   **79**

8 Just Another Brick in the Wall   **93**

9 When the Pain Persists   **107**

10 Locked in a Room With Open Doors   **120**

11 When There's No Way Out   **132**

12 You Have To Get Out of the Boat   **145**

To my grandparents, Otto and Ruth Hansen,
who had a major influence on my life.

Grandpa, pastor, evangelist, and church planter,
went to be with his Lord in 1979.

Nanny is still very much alive at 85.

1

From Frustration to Fulfillment

There they were, dangling from the ignition switch of my car, sealed off from my grasp by locked doors and closed windows. I had done it again! In my eagerness to show off my new car to a friend, I had hurried out the door without the keys. Rats!

"Well," I said to myself, "I'll just try the old wire-hanger-through-the-crack-in-the-window trick." Forty-five minutes later I resigned myself to the fact that I wasn't going to get the hanger through the crack in the window because there was no crack in the window to get it through. Just before climbing out of my car, I had rolled the windows up tight to make sure no one could steal it.

But wait. I had an extra key in my wallet! Where did I put my wallet? No . . . I couldn't have! Yes . . . I did. Because we planned to go to the beach, I had driven to my friend's house wearing my swimming trunks. My wallet was in the back pocket of my pants, which were locked safely in my car.

Most of us don't need to go back very far to recall the last time we felt frustrated. Examples come quickly to mind.

Frustration is . . .

● a woman spilling coffee on her new white dress five minutes after arriving at the restaurant.

7

- a driver on his way to work, wedged in traffic between an overloaded truck and a beat-up Volkswagen.
- a secretary who can't find the reports she just finished typing.
- a husband who doesn't remember where he is supposed to meet his wife for lunch.
- a housewife watching her five children and one dog track mud on her newly cleaned carpet.
- an employee hoping to please a boss who won't be pleased.
- an insomniac trying to recall the words to a song that runs endlessly through his head.
- a shopper who can't remember where her car is parked.
- an avid football fan watching his team do everything wrong.
- an adult who can't figure out how to open a "kid-proofed" aspirin bottle.

King Solomon wrote, "Hope deferred makes the heart sick, but desire fulfilled is a tree of life" (Prov. 13:12). No matter what form they come in, frustrations are always irritating, even when they only result in a little added inconvenience or an extra trip to the school to pick up the child we forgot on the first run. But sometimes frustrations do more than merely try our daily dose of patience. Deferred hopes and frustrated desires can make us sick at heart. They can gnaw at us, sapping our energy and enthusiasm, and our enjoyment of life.

According to the dictionary, *frustrate* means "to prevent from achieving a goal or gratifying a desire." Pulsing through each one of us are a number of keenly felt, God-given desires. We desire to be intimate with another person, to love and be loved, to have at least one other person with whom we can share our whole self. We desire to be successful, whatever that might mean for us, to achieve something significant in our vocation or avocation. We desire to feel confident in ourselves, to be accepting of how we look, and what we are doing with our lives. We desire to experience meaning and purpose in our jobs and our everyday lives. We desire to be free, to be content. We desire to be at peace with the past and to live unafraid of the future.

But more often than seems fair, our desires go unfulfilled. Our dreams and hopes and goals are thwarted by some obnoxious frustration, leaving us perplexed, empty, and broken. Loneliness frustrates our urge for intimacy. Boredom frustrates our ache for meaning. Rejection, failure, and insecurity frustrate our longing to love and accept ourselves as the unique, valuable individuals we'd like to believe we are.

Ann

With just a few years left before she retired from teaching, Ann felt on top of the world. She and her engineer husband had been married for 25 years and were more in love than ever. Her children were grown, the last one having just left the nest. As much as she liked teaching, she was looking forward to the time when she and Ted would have more time to enjoy their home and to travel.

Then Ann learned that she had cancer. Within a week, her entire world changed. The tomorrows she had planned on didn't look rosy anymore. She wasn't even sure how many tomorrows she would have.

Besides her fear and pain, Ann found some other things happening to her that she never would have imagined. Even though her husband was always right there with her in the hospital, and despite the mountains of mail that assured her of her friends' support, Ann couldn't help but feel alone. The cancer seemed to cut her off from everyone else, as though she were a criminal sentenced to solitary confinement.

And even though she knew she hadn't caused the cancer that was victimizing her body, she found herself actually feeling guilty, for not taking better care of herself, for ruining their vacation plans, and for causing her husband so much grief and bother.

Yet most of all, Ann felt frustrated. Frustrated that she didn't know whether she was going to live for another 30 years or die the next week. Frustrated that she couldn't do more to get well. Frustrated that her husband's love and encouragement didn't seem to be enough. Frustrated that something so awful had happened to her, when other people hadn't been sick a day in their lives. Frustrated because she didn't understand everything the doctors told her or why they were doing what they were.

Ann's frustrations—of guilt, fear, loneliness, and confusion—are common to all of us, to one degree or another. For 60 Americans each day, these frustrations prove to be more than they can handle, prompting them to take their own lives. Four to five times that number in the U.S. attempt suicide each day. In 1978, the President's Commission on Mental Health estimated that one out of every seven Americans will at some time require professional treatment for emotional disturbance. Currently, almost 55 million Americans are suffering from mild to moderate depression. The 1980 statistics show that 48 out of every 100 marriages in the U.S. end in divorce, a testimony in part to the severity of frustrations many people encounter in living with a partner. On the other hand, the single one-third of the adult population in the U.S.—whether never married, divorced, or widowed—would be quick to point out to those who are married that singleness has its frustrations as well. If you are feeling frustrated, you are not alone.

Three Facts About Frustration

As a person all too familiar with frustration, as a counselor who has heard the pain of frustration vividly described and who has seen it in living color, and as a pastor whose goal it is to give hope and courage to frustrated people week after week, I have learned some very important truths about this foe called frustration.

• First, I have learned that we will never be totally free of frustration as long as we live on this earth. It is a fact of our existence, just because there is disease, because there is inflation, because there are machines that rust and break down, and because there are stubborn people who don't have the wisdom to always agree with our opinions. Jesus plainly informed His disciples that as long as they lived in the world they would have tribulation (John 16:33). What did He mean by tribulation? Pressure, affliction, travail, anguish, difficulty, oppression. Put them all together and they spell FRUSTRATION.

After learning this rather less-than-thrilling lesson, I asked, "Why? Why, if God wants us to be fulfilled, as He said He does (see John 10:10), does He allow us to be so frustrated? Why, since He's given us the desire for intimacy and for achievement, does He allow those desires to be thwarted?"

After much thought and study, and after asking as many people as I could, I finally reached this profound conclusion: I'm not sure.

Oh, I have some ideas, and so does most everyone else. But none of us knows for *sure* why God allows the people He created and loves to experience so much pain and frustration.

● But even though I don't know for sure *why* God allows frustrations to come into our lives, I know that often the result of frustration is that we are better people for it. Frustration is not an evil to be avoided at all costs. Rather it is a teacher from whom we can learn much.

A friend once told me that certain qualities in our lives can be developed only during periods of pain and frustration. Patience, for example, is produced under conditions in which our natural reaction is impatience. Patience can be developed when your husband is late for dinner—again. Or when your wife overdraws the checking account—again. Without frustration, there can be no patience. Frustration can be an effective agent in helping us to become better people, even though we don't know for sure why God allows our circumstances to get so fouled up.

● But I also learned one more very important truth. No matter how frustrated I may be, there is always hope. Frustration need not be the period at the end of the sentence. It is only the comma that forces us to stop and take a breath. Frustration need not be final. Failure can be the back door to success. Obstacles can become opportunities, scars can turn into stars. Frustration and futility can develop into freedom and fulfillment.

Good News

All very fine. But *how* does it happen? The message of the New Testament is called the Gospel. The word *Gospel* means "good news." There is a great difference between giving someone good advice and giving him good news. To give a drowning swimmer good advice on how to swim better would be heartless. What he needs is help. What he needs is strength, and someone to rescue him. A prisoner in jail may benefit from some good advice on "How to Cope While Serving a Life Sentence." But I'm sure he would prefer to hear the good news that he had been pardoned.

The Gospel of Jesus Christ is more than good advice. It is good news! It is strength for the swimmer and pardon for the prisoner. It is a message of love for the lonely, of hope for the dejected, of grace for the guilty, of meaning for the bored. The Gospel is not just advice; it is power: "For I am not ashamed of the Gospel; for it is the power of God for salvation to everyone who believes" (Rom. 1:16). The Gospel is the good news that Jesus Christ has made it possible for the frustrated, the hurt, and the hopeless to experience healing and fulfillment.

Because we enjoy children, my wife and I baby-sit a ten-month-old boy named Robert for a few hours every Saturday. One of the things that Robert discovered the first time his parents dropped him off at our home, was the stairway. Without hesitation he shifted into fourth gear and motored over to the bottom of the stairs from the middle of the living room where we had set him down. As he began the imposing task of climbing all 13 stairs, my wife—playing the role of the concerned mother—kindly ordered me to make sure that

Robert didn't fall and hurt himself. I got down on my knees and began climbing the steps one by one with Robert, my hand strategically positioned just behind him to prevent an accident.

But Robert had climbed steps before and was more than equal to the challenge. He polished off the first flight of stairs without much difficulty and began climbing the second flight without a bat of his long eyelashes.

But with three steps to go, Robert began to waver. His enthusiasm hadn't dampened a bit—that contagious smile of his still glowed from his face—but his legs and arms no longer moved as quickly or as assertively. He climbed two more stairs with great effort, stopping to rest with just one more to go.

After a short break to measure his final hurdle, Robert gathered himself together and with all the determination of an Olympian he stretched and struggled to haul his little body over that last step. He couldn't make it. His arms and legs just didn't have enough left in them to finish the task.

With an anguished look Robert glanced over at me. I smiled and said, "C'mon Robert, you can make it!"

Like a prizefighter answering the bell for the last round, Robert gathered himself for one more attempt. His weary muscles went through the motions, but again Robert faltered and began to fall back. But this time there was a difference—I placed my hand on his behind, and gave him a boost. Success! With a squeal of triumph Robert shot me a look of thanks, and dashed off with a new burst of energy to explore the exciting new world of upstairs he had been waiting to drool on.

We don't need anyone to tell us that life can be very frustrating. Sometimes when we give it our very best shot, we still fall short of our dreams and desires.

But frustration need not be the last word. When it seems that our last chance has been used up and all of our strength and energy is gone, along comes the Gospel of Jesus Christ to give us that boost of power we need.

For the Gospel is more than a manual on how to climb the stairs. It is the power to climb them. The Gospel is more than an offer of sympathy for those who hurt. It is salve, a balm to heal the hurt.

Yes, we will always have frustrations in life, all of us, even "supersaints" if there are any. But frustration need not have the last word, ever! The Apostle Paul writes, "And we know that God causes *all* things to work together for good to those who love God" (Rom. 8:28). God is able to cause *all* things to develop into something good. He is able to take the most painful, perplexing, frustrating experience and transform it into something fulfilling.

This book will tell you how you can work together with God to turn your frustrations into fulfillment. It will show you what you can do to turn the lemons of your life into lemonade. And it will remind you of what God has promised to do to turn your groans into growth.

Before the butterfly is a caterpillar. Before a resurrection comes death. Before fulfillment, there often is frustration. But take heart—frustration is not the last word!

2

When You've Got the Guilties

I hung up the phone. Paralyzed by the impact of what I had just heard, I sat riveted to my chair, my ears and face glowing with emotion. For 45 minutes, a man I had never met had loudly reproached me for something of which I was innocent. If his goal was to make me feel guilty, he certainly succeeded.

A few months before, this man's wife had come into my office for counseling. We spent an hour together, in which I mostly listened to her spill out her frustrations over her marriage. At the end of the session I shared with her a few insights that I had learned from the Bible and from my own marriage, prayed with her, and encouraged her to get in touch with me soon. I suggested she ask her husband if he would be willing to come in with her. A week later I made a brief follow-up phone call, and then never heard from her again.

Now this very hurt and angry man had called to accuse me of causing their divorce. He insisted that his wife had never thought of divorcing him before she talked to me, that I must have put the idea into her head, and therefore was responsible for her leaving him. Although I assured him that I had not encouraged his wife to divorce him but rather had told her very optimistically that I believed there was a great deal of hope for their marriage, nothing was effective in calming him. Finally, sensing our conversation was counterproductive, I managed to excuse myself and hang up.

I was innocent, I told myself. How could he blame me for his divorce, when I had talked with his wife for only an hour? It was crazy! The best thing was to just forget the whole mess!

But I couldn't. All night I stared at the ceiling, churning inside like a volcano preparing to erupt. Try as I might, I could not erase the guilt that had infested my mind. My head told me I was innocent and I believed it, but my heart still hadn't gotten the message.

Guilt can be as painful and crippling an emotion as there is. Every time he gets into a car, Jim is haunted by the memory of his accident. Four years ago his friend, who was riding with him to a baseball game, had his legs crushed by a car Jim collided with. His friend would never walk again, and Jim could not forget it.

Patty smiled as she held her neighbor's new baby, but she broke into tears as soon as she reached the privacy of her own bedroom. Even though she and Bill had decided that they couldn't afford another child with three already, Patty still felt a nagging guilt over the abortion she had last year. If only there were something she could do to forget the whole awful experience.

Guilt Described

Guilt is the frustration of our God-given desire to be at peace with God, with our friends and families, and with ourselves. Guilt is the inevitable feeling that floods our conscience when we fail to live up to our values and convictions.

The deepest source of human misery is guilt. O. Hobart Mowrer tells us,

> From many quarters now comes reaffirmation of the view that man is preeminently a social being and that for him the supreme anguish comes not from bodily deprivation or pain, but from the rupturing of his sociality which

we broadly denote by the word sin or alienation. . . . Increasingly it appears that the central fact in personality disorder is real guilt (*The Crisis in Psychiatry and Religion,* D. Van Nostrand Company, Inc.; pp. 167, 217).

For many people, guilt is more than a nuisance. It is a probing, searing pain.

Vernon Grounds, former president of Denver Seminary, describes guilt in this way:

Guilt is a very curious phenomenon—that unavoidable feeling of self-condemnation which a person experiences when he fails to do what he believes is right or when he voluntarily does what he believes is wrong. That feeling is accompanied by the fear of punishment for failure to obey conscience, and yet a sense that the punishment is justified (*Emotional Problems and the Gospel,* Zondervan, p. 91).

As Grounds points out, the feeling of guilt is a bit of a paradox. On one hand, it is a fear that we will be punished for our sin; and yet on the other hand, it is the feeling that we ought to be punished.

Do you remember those times as a youngster when you had done something wrong but your parents had not yet discovered your crime? Perhaps you broke a lamp while innocently wrestling with your brother, or stole some cookies and spoiled your appetite for dinner. All afternoon you waited for your mom or your dad to come home from shopping or from work and find out your misdeed. You shook with fear as you envisioned the awful punishment that they would inflict on your delicate little body. But your parents came home and nothing was said. Your mind quickly calculated that their silence could be attributed to one of two reasons: either they had not discovered the crime yet, or they had discovered it but were not saying anything because they wanted to make you suffer a little longer. Knowing the great lengths the twisted adult mind could go to make you miserable, you assumed that the latter reason was the case.

Finally, after suffering silently through most of dinner, you could stand it no longer. You broke down and confessed your crime. And to relieve your troubled conscience, you asked for the only thing that could make up for what you had done—punishment: "I did it, I did it! I broke the lamp! Go ahead, beat me! Throw me out of the house, make me eat spinach and liver for a week, just do something!" Guilt is the fear of being punished for our sin, yet the feeling that punishment is deserved.

In their book *Freedom From Guilt,* Bruce Narramore and Bill Counts suggest that guilt is made up of three basic feelings or attitudes. The first is a fear of punishment. The second is a feeling of depression, of worthlessness, and lowered self-esteem. It is impossible to feel good about ourselves when we are feeling guilty. The third basic attitude or feeling is a fear of isolation and rejection. Through the years we have learned to assume that if we don't measure up to people's standards, we will be rejected by them (Harvest House, p. 19).

The Destructiveness of Guilt

From the preceding descriptions of how guilt is experienced, it is apparent that guilt is destructive. According to Narramore and Counts, "feelings of psychological guilt are always destructive" (p. 36).

• Guilt destroys self-confidence and self-esteem. It tears down our image of ourselves until we think of ourselves as horrible, unworthy, wretched people.

• Guilt destroys relationships. A person who feels guilty tends to focus on himself, and on how he can make up for his failures, his misery, or his inadequacy. A person focused on self soon destroys whatever supportive relationships he may have. Guilty people aren't much fun to be around. It's hard to have a relationship with someone whose eyeballs look only inward.

• Guilt destroys by prohibiting growth. A person who feels guilty is focused not on the future and on how he might grow, but on the past. Daniel Levinson, author of *The Seasons of a Man's Life,* is a pioneer in the study of the developmental stages of adulthood. He has concluded that before a man can move on in life, before he can mature, before he can take the next step up the developmental ladder, it is imperative for him to somehow come to peace with the guilts of his past (Ballantine Books, p. 223ff). A person trying to drive down the street won't get very far if he spends his whole time looking over his shoulder. Neither will the person absorbed with his guilt make much progress in personal growth, as long as he remains fixated by his past.

● But perhaps the most destructive effect of guilt is that instead of drawing us to God—the only One able to effectually relieve our guilt—it drives us away from God. In *The Mind Changers,* Em Griffen observes that when someone makes us feel guilty, we have a tendency to avoid him in the future (Tyndale, p. 63).

The only time in my life that I ever stole anything was as a six-year-old, when I gave into my obsession for chocolate bunnies. Not being a very competent crook, I was easily spotted by the owner of the local grocery store who knew me well and promptly called my mother. When I learned that I had been discovered I felt so guilty that I was never again able to go into that store when the grocer was there.

Instead of motivating us to seek out God and His forgiveness, our feelings of guilt more often influence us to turn away from God. It is only human to avoid people who remind us of our shortcomings and who resurrect in us all the negative emotions that we've tried so hard to cover up. Thus while God is the only One able to deliver us from our guilt, we are driven by that very guilt to avoid God at all costs.

Deliverance From Guilt

For those of us who ache to be at peace but find ourselves frustrated by guilt, there is good news! The destructive power of guilt can be broken. God is able to deliver us from our guilt and to set us at peace with Himself, with ourselves, and with others.

But how? Most likely you've heard before that God can forgive your sins, that there is grace for your guilt. But you also know that you still feel guilty. So what's next?

The way out of the grimy grasp of guilt is illustrated for us in the unique story of Jesus' encounter with a prostitute. It pictures two key realities that we need to face, two truths we need to remind ourselves of, in order to experience freedom from guilt.

There are three main characters in this particular story told by Luke—a prostitute, Simon the Pharisee, and Jesus. Let us look at this passage in Luke 7 through the eyes of Simon. As a Pharisee, Simon knew the Law of God backward and forward, and had most likely kept it as well as anyone. He was a religious leader, highly respected in the community. Now Simon invited Jesus, a man many were proclaiming as a prophet, to have dinner with him:

And behold, there was a woman in the city who was a sinner; and when she learned that He was reclining at table in the Pharisee's house, she brought an alabaster vial of perfume, and standing behind Him at His feet, weeping, she began to wet His feet with her tears, and kept wiping them with the hair of her head, and kissing His feet, and anointing them with the perfume (Luke 7:37-38).

Simon was astounded by the whole scene! He said to himself, "If this man were a prophet He would know who and what sort of person this woman is who is touching Him, that she is a sinner" (v. 39).

Jesus knew what Simon was thinking and attempted to enlighten him by telling him a parable.

"A certain money lender had two debtors; one owed five hundred denarii, and the other fifty. When they were unable to pay, he graciously forgave them both. Which of them therefore will love him more?" Simon answered

and said, "I supposed the one whom he forgave more."
And He said to him, 'You have judged correctly'" (vv.
41-43).

Then Jesus turned Simon's attention to the woman as
He said:

"Do you see this woman? I entered your house; you
gave Me no water for My feet, but she has wet My feet
with her tears, and wiped them with her hair. You gave
Me no kiss; but she, since the time I came in, has not
ceased to kiss My feet. You did not anoint My head with
oil, but she has anointed My feet with perfume. For this
reason I say to you, her sins, which are many, have been
forgiven, for she loved much; but he who is forgiven little,
loves little" (vv. 44-47).

What is the point of this story? That the person who has
sinned more is then forgiven more, and so loves God more? If
so, we should all go out and commit the sins we have always
wanted to, so that God can forgive us and we can love Him all
the more!

The real point of the story is this: Because the sinful woman
was so aware of her own failure to live as she knew she
should, she was able to more fully experience the forgiveness
of God, and through her *experience of God's forgiveness* she
was able to love much.

The woman knew she was a sinner. No one needed to point
that out to her. The fact that she approached Jesus as she
did—with tears and humility, wiping His feet with her hair,
pouring ointment on His feet—vividly demonstrated her own
sense of unworthiness. In contrast, Simon revealed his smug-
ness and self-righteousness by doing none of the tasks ex-
pected of a host—Simon was unwilling to face the reality that
he too was a failure before God.

In the *Good News Bible,* the point of the passage is made
clearer: "I tell you, then, the great love she has shown proves
that her many sins have been forgiven. But whoever has been
forgiven little shows only a little love" (v. 47). In other words, a

person's capacity to love himself, to love others, and especially to love God is directly related to his experience of God's forgiveness.

The first truth this passage reminds us of is that we are in a very real sense *failures*. Obviously, that is not good news. It is something we would rather forget about ourselves. In fact, it seems like the very thing we are supposed to forget. But the reality is that if we are to experience the healing, restoring forgiveness of God, it is something we cannot forget. Before we can be free from guilt, we must face our failures.

Sin Can't Be Covered Up

When something embarrassing happens to us, we try hard to act natural, in order to not call further attention to ourselves. We want to cover our embarrassment. Much to my consternation, I have never been able to do that. Whenever I get excited or embarrassed, my face glows as brightly as Rudolph's red nose. And the more people notice how red my cheeks are and how embarrassed I am, the redder I get. How I wish that I had some way of draining the color out of my face so that people wouldn't realize how embarrassed I am!

Just as it's natural to want to cover up discomfort, so it is very natural to want to cover up sin and failure. We would prefer to forget the time long ago when we got caught drawing pictures on the wall, not so much because we did something wrong as because we got caught. We would rather sweep under the rug all those times we found ourselves being impatient and moody and bitter and selfish. We would be willing to do almost anything to erase the memory of that sin, that mistake, that embarrassment that has caused us so much pain and guilt.

But unfortunately, trying to cover up our sins doesn't really help. For we are very much aware of what we have done, and so is God. Covering up doesn't get rid of the guilt; it just keeps it hanging around longer.

When David learned that covering up sin didn't help matters

any, he wrote, "When I kept silent about my sin, my body wasted away through my groaning all day long. For day and night Thy hand was heavy upon me; my vitality was drained away as with the fever-heat of summer" (Ps. 32:3-4). I know just what David was talking about, that heaviness that feels like a bag of cement laid across my chest, the loss of energy, the feeling of wasting away, of groaning because of twinges of guilt shooting continuously through my conscience.

But David learned his lesson well: "I acknowledged my sin to Thee, and I did not hide my iniquity; I said, 'I will confess my transgressions to the Lord'; then Thou didst forgive the guilt of my sin" (v. 5). When David admitted his fault, his mistake, his sin, then God forgave him and relieved him from the misery of his guilt.

Guilt or Godly Grief?

Does God want us to feel guilty? Does God want us to have a fear of punishment, to feel worthless, to feel rejected? No! God never wants us to feel that kind of guilt, even when we've broken His laws. God desires that we experience what Paul called "godly grief." Look at Paul's explanation:

For even if I made you sorry with my letter, I do not regret it (though I did regret it), for I see that the letter grieved you, though only for a while. As it is, I rejoice, not because you were grieved, but because you were grieved into repenting; for you felt a godly grief, so that you suffered no loss through us. For godly grief produces a repentance that leads to salvation and brings no regret, but worldly grief produces death (2 Cor. 7:8-10, RSV).

Godly grief is a sorrow over sin that motivates us to repent, to actively renounce our sins and turn to God for forgiveness. Guilt, or worldly grief, leads to death. It is destructive, not constructive. God does not desire that we feel guilty in this sense. Rather He desires that we experience a godly grief that faces our failure and sin and will lead to repentance and confession.

Feeling Forgiven

In order to experience God's healing forgiveness, we must remind ourselves that we are failures. Before we can be forgiven, we must face our sin head on, confess it to God, and repent and turn away from our sin.

There is another truth that we need to be reminded of. Most of us are very aware of our failures. We are reminded of them too often by books and sermons and family members to ever possibly forget them. What most of us need to be reminded of is that we are *forgiven*.

When I was growing up we had a small dog named Toby. Toby was generally a good dog, but on occasion when we would be out for a walk, he would get the itch to take off for new territory. All of a sudden Toby would just shoot off, with me running behind yelling threats at him. But he would pay absolutely no attention. I knew very well that when he came back he would try to convince me that he hadn't heard me, though I knew he had. But when Toby would come home a couple of hours later and I would see him and gruffly call him over to me, he would know he was guilty. He would put his tail between his legs, plaster his ears back, and droopingly saunter over to me, walking slower and slower until just when he got to me he would roll over on his back and beg for mercy. I never could bring myself to punish him!

Many of us feel just like Toby did. We know very well that we are guilty, and we live our lives smothered by a shroud of guilt. We allow that guilt to eat away at us, to rob us of our sense of peace and well-being, to deprive us of our sleep and energy, and to strip us of our creativity and self-confidence.

Unavailing Attempts at Absolution

What do you do when you feel guilty? Do you attempt to absolve yourself of your guilt feelings by trying harder to be good or to perform perfectly? If so, you may have learned that it doesn't work. Instead of ridding yourself of your guilt, you find yourself caught in the trap of perfectionism.

John Powell describes the perfectionist in his book, *The Secret of Staying in Love*: "Such a person is driven to do whatever he attempts with meticulous perfection. Performance is the assumed condition for recognition and love; so his performance becomes crucially important. He is always trying to pass the test, pay the price of admission into a feeling of personal worth" (Argus, p. 23).

God *does* call us to be holy. But the perfectionist goes beyond that. Perfectionism is a disease because it causes us to feel guilty about matters for which we need not feel guilty. Many of us have been brought up to believe that to be loved and accepted by our friends, family, and even by God, we have to be perfect. Built into each of us is what psychologists call the "ideal self," that perfect image of you. The ideal self never makes a mistake. The ideal self always gets A's, always says the clever and appropriate thing, is never clumsy, never has a hair out of place, and is always on time. But the problem is that the real self never measures up to the ideal self. The real self is clumsy. The real self sometimes forgets to put water into the car battery and the battery goes dead. The real self spills hot fudge on new white slacks.

Clumsiness is not a sin! We are conditioned to think it is, though, because as kids we were always scolded and punished for being clumsy. Did you ever have this scene take place in your home? You are around the table eating dinner. It is hot and muggy and everyone is tired from a long day. The youngest in the family reaches across the table and clumsily knocks over the milk. The father bellows, "You dumb kid, what did you spill your milk for?" And to emphasize the point, he reaches over and lightly raps the poor kid on the side of the head. At our dinner table things were always being spilled, and the scene I just described was repeated so often that when we did spill anything, our first reaction was to duck!

Many of us live like that. When we do something less than perfect we instinctively duck because we think God is upset with us. But the truth is that God is not upset with us. Those kinds of things are not particularly crucial to God. To be clumsy, to make mistakes, to be less than the "ideal self" is not sin. It is being human. It is part of who we are as God's finite and limited creatures.

In coming to terms with myself—after the conversation with the irate husband I described at the beginning of this chapter—I had to remind myself that as much as I might wish I were a perfect counselor and pastor, I am not. As much as I wish I could save every marriage or always have the perfect answers, I can't. I do my very best, but even my best will fall short of pleasing everyone. But I am learning that this is OK. God doesn't expect me to be all-knowing and all-wise. In the nonmoral areas of life, my best is good enough. Trying to be perfect doesn't make my guilt go away. It only makes it worse.

Another way we try to absolve ourselves of guilt is by punishing ourselves. Since part of guilt is a feeling that punishment is deserved, we reason that if we punish ourselves we will get rid of our guilt. So we punish ourselves by continuing to feel guilty, by rehashing over and over again the source of our guilt. We punish ourselves by fretting and fuming and becoming more depressed, thinking that we are too awful to feel good or enjoy life.

Brigham Young, one of the founders of the Mormon faith, taught an exaggerated equivalent to our propensity for punishing ourselves when we feel guilty. In the *Journal of Discourses* Young wrote:

Suppose you found your brother in bed with your wife, and put a javelin through both of them, you would be justified, and they would atone for their sins, and be received into the kingdom of God. . . . There is not a man or woman, who violates the covenants made with their God, that will not be required to pay the debt. The blood of Christ will never wipe that out, your own blood must atone for it" (Quoted by Walter Martin in *The Kingdom of the Cults*, Bethany, p. 192).

By punishing ourselves, we think we can atone for our sins and be absolved of our guilt. But it doesn't work.

The Reassuring Reality

The reality we so desperately need to be reminded of is that Jesus has already taken all the punishment for us in His death on the cross. According to the Bible, Jesus is the only person qualified to die for the sins of another, because only Jesus is perfect Himself. And contrary to Brigham Young, His blood *is* enough to atone for our sins. If we have faced our failures, confessed our sin, and repented, then we can *know*—whether we *feel* it or not—that we *are* forgiven! God no longer holds anything against us. There are no debts left to pay.

Most of us are not like Simon the Pharisee in Luke's story. We are more like the sinful woman who knew so well that she had failed. And like her we need to hear the words spoken by Jesus, "Your sins are forgiven."

We who are haunted by guilt need to grasp the reality that once we have put our faith in Jesus Christ, God is not our accuser. He is not pointing His finger at us with a frown on His face. But if God isn't the one accusing us, who is? Where is all this guilt coming from, if not from God?

We see an answer to that question in the Book of Revelation. Satan is the accuser who night and day points the finger at us, shaming us and telling us that we are guilty, that we deserve to be punished and despised for our weakness. (See Rev. 12:10.)

But Satan is wrong. We need not punish ourselves anymore. God does not want us to flagellate ourselves when we fail. He does not want us to denigrate ourselves when we sin. Jesus Christ has already been punished for us. He was degraded and insulted for us. He was put to death for us. No more blood is necessary. No more pain, no more depression, no more sleepless nights are required. There is nothing more we can do, even if we wanted to. The only thing that God accepts as payment for our sin is the blood of someone perfect and holy, and that has already been given. Jesus paid it all!

Forgiveness Is Forgetting

A few winters ago on a rather cold weekend, I took our church youth group on a ski trip. On Saturday morning after I heard the weather report I came back into the cabin, announced that it was 15 degrees *below* zero, and encouraged everyone to dress warmly. One girl took me quite seriously and spent the next 20 minutes putting on every article of clothing she had with her. After a final check to insure that no part of her body was exposed, she pronounced herself ready and strode out to the slopes. Five minutes later she snuck back into the cabin and sheepishly confessed, "I forgot my skis."

That girl was so concerned with the cold that she forgot the most essential part of her ski equipment. Many of us become so absorbed with our sins and our failures that we forget the most basic factor in our relationship with God—that we are forgiven. So much of our energy and thought is focused on our failures that we have little or none left to focus on loving God and enjoying our relationship with Him.

How can we be free from the frustration of guilt? First, we must face our sin, respond with a godly grief, and repent. Then, when we have remembered to face our failures, we must remember to forget them. Why remember what God has forgotten?

"I, I am He who blots out your transgressions for My own sake, and I will not remember your sins" (Isa. 43:25).

When you have faced your failures, then forget them. God already has!

3

Alone Again

For some reasons my loneliest moments have always involved snow. Maybe that is because I grew up in Minnesota and so many moments of any kind involved snow. Perhaps snow is symbolic of some great cosmic truth. Or maybe it just worked out that way.

As an adolescent I was basically a loner. My favorite social activity was walking my dog. I especially enjoyed taking Toby out in the winter, when the drifts of snow were so deep that Toby's walking consisted of jumping from one footprint to another, as I blazed a trail through the backyard and up the hill overlooking our house. Yet as I stood in the quiet under the large misshapen tree that crowned the hill we had just climbed, I could not help but be struck with a twinge of loneliness when I realized that my most intimate companion was the furry creature that lay panting and shivering at my feet.

Christmas was always an especially festive time for our family, full of laughter and food, presents and singing. Each year we would load up our car with gifts and drive through the glistening snow that wrapped the city in a blanket of white, to spend Christmas Eve at Grandmother's house. But one particular Christmas, in 1975, only four of the nine who had gathered in 1974 were present. My father had died of a heart attack. My grandmother's sister had died in a rest home. My grandfather had suffered a major stroke and could no longer provide the strong leadership that he had given us for so many years as a minister and as a patriarch. My one brother and his wife had moved to Canada, and my other brother was unable to make it that night because of work. We sang the old carols, ate the Christmas cookies, opened the presents, and prayed to our Lord. But the emptiness each of us felt hung like a cloud over the whole evening.

Four years later I was traveling in the western United States, visiting some friends. It was March and I was glad to leave the cold and the snow of Minnesota. Driving from Grand Junction, Colorado to Sante Fe, New Mexico, I discovered that snow does not confine itself to the great Midwest. As I curled through the Rocky Mountains I ran head-on into one of the fiercest blizzards I had ever seen. After battling the thick, wet snow that seemed to erase all color from my sight, I finally stopped the car and decided to wait it out. Accompanying the loneliness that comes with being stranded on a mountain in a snowstorm is another emotion—fear. It was then, however, that I suddenly experienced a deep spiritual awakening. For as I sat there, a voice revealed to me a cure for my loneliness. At first I thought I was imagining, but as I listened the inner voice became more insistent. Its message to me was simple but profound; "Move to California!" Three months later I moved to California.

When Christmas of my first winter in San Jose rolled around, and for the first time I was away from my own family and close friends, I realized that even people in California can be lonely.

And I never missed snow so much in my life.

When It Hurts To Be Alone

Loneliness belongs to all of us. It is not the exclusive domain of the person who lives alone or the traveling salesperson. Loneliness is common property.

Some have even named loneliness the number-one problem in America. Dr. Billy Graham called it the most pervasive problem he has encountered. Dr. Carin Rubenstein, a social psychologist at New York University, asserts that more than a quarter of all Americans, over 50 million people, are "painfully lonely." A survey of 40,000 readers of *Psychology Today* revealed that 67 percent of all men and women often feel lonely, while 79 percent of those under 18 say they often feel lonely. Dr. James Lynch, Scientific Director of Psychosomatic Clinics at the University of Maryland School of Medicine declares,

Loneliness is the major contributor to disease—mental and physical—in our society. The statistics are awesome. It cuts across all ages. Loneliness is a very depressive condition, and if it is serious enough, people who are lonely will destroy themselves (Quoted in "Loneliness Is the Number One Problem in America" by George Hunter, *National Enquirer*, March 1980).

Loneliness can indeed cause people to destroy themselves. Dr. Armand Nicholi, a noted psychologist suggests this:

Loneliness is an extremely painful and frightening human experience—so painful that modern psychiatry has pretty much avoided the study of it. Today's drug addicts, alcoholics, workaholics, and even psychotics may in large measure be attempting to avoid the pain of loneliness ("The Fractured Family: Following It into the Future," *Christianity Today*, May 25, 1979).

Loneliness can also drive people to compromise their own moral standards. For such people, anything is better than the continuing agony of being alone. A church in Southern California took a survey of their singles' group and discovered that out of 203 people, only 45 had managed to resist the temptation of immorality. When asked to list their reasons for having sexual relations despite their convictions against it, these 158 unmarried Christians listed loneliness as the overwhelming single reason (Harold Ivan Smith, "Sex and Singleness the Second Time Around," *Christianity Today*, May 25, 1979).

What is loneliness? Gary Collins, author of *How To Be a People-Helper*, defines it as "the painful awareness that we lack meaningful contact with others" ("Gary Collins on Loneliness," *Voices*, Trinity Evangelical Divinity School, Fall 1978, p. 8).

Bill Moulder distinguishes between loneliness and solitude. Solitude is a positive time of refreshment and renewal. Loneliness is the painful experience of wanting to be with others but being unable to. Moulder describes loneliness in this way:

What does it feel like to be lonely? I think the word that best describes the experience for me is *empty*. It feels as if there were a big hole right in the middle of my chest. Sometimes it is a dull pain, a listlessness. Even that which I enjoy most—a walk in the woods, a Bruckner symphony—seems pointless, even painful because I respond to it by wanting to share it, and when I reach out to share it there is no one there" ("Living Alone," *Voices*, Fall 1978, pp. 4-5).

Some of us are driven by loneliness to do things we otherwise would not do—to drink compulsively, to eat compulsively, or to work compulsively. Some of us do nothing. For we have simply learned to accept loneliness as a way of life.

But there is hope. While loneliness is a painful and very prevalent ailment, it is not incurable. God can enable us to turn any frustration into a fulfilling experience. The frustration of loneliness is no exception.

Jeremiah—The Lonely Prophet

Before examining God's "scratch" for my itch and yours, let us see how He scratched the itch of the man who was probably the loneliest person in the Bible, the Prophet Jeremiah. Perhaps you have heard Jeremiah described as the "weeping prophet" and decided not to take time to read all 52 chapters of his book, since he sounded like a rather depressing person.

The Book of Jeremiah *is* depressing. There is not much good news in it. Little is said about God's mercy or love and not much hope is given. About 622 B.C. God called on Jeremiah to tell the people of Judah that they were about to be thoroughly trounced—not a very pleasant message.

What had happened was this. Sometime after the glorious years of Israel under King David and his son, Solomon, the nation of Israel split into a Northern Kingdom—Israel—and a Southern Kingdom—Judah. Israel lasted until the year 722 B.C. when it was crushed by the nation of Assyria. Jeremiah lived about 100 years later in the nation of Judah, the Southern Kingdom.

Now the people of Judah felt quite smug about the fact that they had outlasted Israel, and were very confident that they would never be defeated, even though they were presently under a good deal of pressure from Egypt and Babylon. Their prophets assured them that they could never fall because the temple of the Lord was in Jerusalem and surely God would not allow a heathen nation to destroy the temple!

Then along came Jeremiah with quite a different message. For God instructed Jeremiah to tell the people of Judah that time was running out on them, that He had had enough of their deceitfulness and their pride, and was about to judge them just as He had judged Israel 100 years before. In fact, the people of Judah had passed the point of no return. Jeremiah very rarely even bothered to exhort the people of Judah to repent, because it was too late.

Can you visualize Jeremiah's position? He was the only person predicting that Judah would be defeated by Babylon. He sounded like a traitor. Even worse, Jeremiah was considered a heretic. The other prophets had plenty of support for their insistence on the inviolability of the temple. Jeremiah was as much a heretic in his day as a theologian denying the virgin birth of Christ is in ours.

The people did not respond well to Jeremiah. They threw him in jail. They put him in the stocks. They tossed him into a well. On more than one occasion, they tried to kill him. Not once in the 50 years that he prophesied did the people of Judah ever believe him.

Jeremiah was rejected, ignored, scorned, abused, hated, alone, and very lonely. He knew well the agony of loneliness. He remembered too that God had told him at the outset of his career that all of the people would turn on him (Jer. 1:18-19). He remembered how God had forbidden him from getting married (16:1-4). How did Jeremiah respond? His reaction was the same as many of us have had at one time or another—he got angry with God. Listen to Jeremiah's exclamation:

O Lord, Thou knowest;
remember me and visit me,
and take vengeance for me on my persecutors.
In Thy forbearance take me not away;
Know that for Thy sake I bear reproach . . .
I did not sit in the company of merrymakers,
nor did I rejoice;
I sat alone, because Thy hand was upon me,
for Thou hadst filled me with indignation.
Why is my pain unceasing,
my wound incurable,
refusing to be healed?
Wilt Thou be to me like a deceitful brook,
like waters that fail? (Jer. 15:15-18, RSV)

To Jeremiah God seemed like nothing more than a babbling brook, promising him comfort and strength and help but not delivering the goods. Jeremiah ached with the pain of being alone, of having no one to support him and care for his needs. Apparently even God had abandoned him. Jeremiah continued his tirade:

O Lord, Thou has deceived me,
and I was deceived;
Thou art stronger than I,
and Thou hast prevailed.

I have become a laughingstock all the day;
everyone mocks me . . .
Cursed be the day
on which I was born!
The day when my mother bore me,
let it not be blessed! . . .
Why did I come forth from the womb
to see toil and sorrow,
and spend my days in shame? (Jer. 20:7, 14, 18, RSV)

Have you ever felt so bad that you did not think the hurt
would ever go away, that you wished you had never been
born? Have you ever felt deceived or cheated by God? Perhaps you have felt those pangs of hurt but have never expressed them before, even to yourself, because you were
afraid you might make God angry at you or might be committing the unpardonable sin. How grateful I am to Jeremiah
for having the courage to say what he felt, so that I could know
that someone else has hurt as badly as I have! If you are
feeling lonely or confused, tell God! He loves you and is
anxious to show you His love, but often He waits to act until
you cry out to Him in your need and despair.

Notice how God responded to Jeremiah's anguished accu-
sations: "If you return, I will restore you and you shall stand
before Me" (Jer. 15:19, RSV). God's word to Jeremiah was not
one of anger or rebuke. It was a word of comfort and assurance: "Come back to Me, Jeremiah, and I will give you new
energy and new hope and new life."

God continued this comfort, renewing the promise He had
given Jeremiah: "And I will make you to this people a fortified
wall of bronze; they will fight against you, but they shall not
prevail over you, for I am with you, to save you and deliver
you, says the Lord" (v. 20). No matter how alone we may
feel, God is always there. God is always on our side, fighting
for us and caring for us. God's word of comfort to Jeremiah
was, "I am with you."

Is God Enough?

But is God enough? Is it fair to tell the person suffering from severe loneliness, "Trust in the Lord and let Him be your friend"?

To answer that question, it is helpful to briefly consider the causes of loneliness. Each person has individual needs. Not everyone battles with loneliness and not all lonely persons are lonely for the same reason.

There are many reasons why a person may be lonely. A common reason is the loss of a person very near, through death, changing locations, or breaking off a relationship. This is the loneliness of the widow, of the divorced person, of the 16-year-old who just lost his girlfriend to a rival.

There is a loneliness caused by developmental factors. This is the chronic feeling of loneliness experienced by the person whose parents failed early in his life to establish in him a healthy sense of worth, well-being, and belonging. Such a person may never have had the confidence necessary to develop the social skills so helpful in making new friends.

There is the loneliness of making a transition alone: going away to school for the first time, moving to a new town, beginning a new job, or battling a disease. There is the loneliness that is intensified by our affluent technological society. We think we no longer need other people to meet our needs or to entertain us. We have televisions, stereos, microwaves, and computer banking. We live in a society that cherishes independence, individualism, and competition instead of mutuality and community.

There is an existential loneliness, a feeling of insignificance and worthlessness that often strikes the person already dissatisfied with his mundane, routinized existence. This is the loneliness of being cut off from God and alone in the universe. It is a pervading sense of fear and anger and often accompanies the contemplation of one's own death.

The underlying cause of loneliness, in summary, is the frustration of our basic human needs. As humans we have three essential needs. First, we have a need for a relationship with God, our Creator. Second, we have a need to love and be loved. God created us as social creatures, and in order for us to be fulfilled we need to be involved in an intimate, personal way with other people. The third need we have is to be worthwhile to ourselves and to others. We need to have a purpose to our lives, something to give us the sense that existence is meaningful and significant. If any of these three needs is unsatisfied, we will probably experience feelings of loneliness.

Some years ago, I did a research study on housewives, trying to find out what they actually felt about their role. After interviewing quite a number of housewives, I learned that they were basically very happy and fulfilled in their role. But I also learned that two factors caused problems. One problem arose when the husband did not give the wife the love, affection, and help that she needed. In that case her basic need for love was being frustrated. Another problem arose when the housewife began to feel that her job was basically worthless, that she as an individual was insignificant. In that case her basic need for worth was being frustrated.

What was most fascinating to me, however, was that in either case the feeling reported by the woman was that of loneliness! In other words, lack of people and affection in one's life is not the only cause of loneliness. A person who sits in a rest home surrounded by more people than he needs, and who gets all sorts of attention from nurses and from his family who visit him every weekend, will still feel lonesome because he thinks he has nothing to contribute. My grandfather's complaint while he lived in a nursing home was not a lack of people. After 65 years as a pastor, he felt lonely because he was now unable to do anything he considered worthwhile.

For many of us who are lonely, it is not enough to know that God is our friend, as comforting as that is. We also have a need for meaningful relationships and a sense of worth. To cure loneliness, all three of those needs must be met.

Curing Our Loneliness

How do we go about curing our loneliness? Sometimes we learn to almost enjoy our self-pity and pain and are unwilling to do anything to change our situation. But if we are seriously interested in doing something about our hurt, there are three steps we can take.

● The first step relates to our human need to love and be loved. Most of us who feel lonely fall into the trap of waiting for someone to call or write or visit us. We are determined not to take the first step. But this is the wrong approach. Listen to what Jesus said: "Give and it will be given to you; good measure, pressed down, shaken together, running over, they will pour into your lap. For whatever measure you deal out to others, it will be dealt to you in return" (Luke 6:38).

Don't wait for someone to give to you. Give first! Reach out. Be a servant. There is a principle in psychology called the "helper-therapy principle," which says that the person reaching out to help is the one who is helped most. By taking the first step to give to somebody else, you will find that God will give back to you more joy and fulfillment than you have ever experienced!

While I was working at a small church in Alberta, Canada, I wrestled with the dilemma of how to give adequate time to the lonely people who belonged to our church. Ours was an old church with a number of elderly and shut-in members. The solution we devised was to transport the lonely people to the rest homes in the community once every week, to visit the lonely people there. The results were outstanding! Not only were the occupants of the rest homes delighted that someone cared enough to come see them, but the people doing the visiting felt terrific. When they reached out to people in need, God gave back to them "good measure, pressed down, shaken together, running over." Take the initiative—be a friend.

● The second step relates to our need for a sense of worth and meaning. The itch of low self-esteem and the itch of purposelessness are large subjects that deserve scratches of their own. They will be considered in later chapters. But briefly, here are some thoughts.

The Christian needs to continually remind himself that even though he may *feel* worthless, he is not. God considers us precious (Isa. 43:4). He was willing to die for us. We have worth simply because God created us and because we belong to Him.

If we still feel worthless even after we have reminded ourselves that we are not, we should do something about it. We can set some goals for ourselves, we can get involved in meaningful projects through our church or community. We can use our hands and build something. No matter who we are or what situation we are in, we still have the capacity to do something productive.

Vernon Anderson was a pastor and a missionary to Brazil for many years, until multiple sclerosis advanced to the point that he could no longer be active. For almost a decade Vernon has been confined to a wheelchair and a bed. There is little that he can do for himself now. His speech is slow and somewhat garbled but he has never lost his quick wit.

Despite his severe limitations, Vernon's ministry extends throughout the world. He is committed to the power of prayer, and through his prayers countless lives have been touched. From all across the country people call him to ask for his prayers, because they know that here is a man who will do more than talk with *them* about God. They know that Vernon will talk with *God* about them. Vernon Anderson has a significant purpose in life through the ministry of prayer.

There is a significant purpose for all of our lives or God would already have taken us to heaven. Take the initiative—find your purpose.

• Yet ultimately there is only one Person who can satisfy us and restore us when we are lonely. Unless we find a meaningful relationship with God, no other step we take to cure our loneliness will be of any value. There will always be those times when we, like Jeremiah, will have no one around to support or encourage us. Only God can fully understand how we feel and only He can really scratch our itch effectively; "The heart knows its own bitterness, and a stranger does not share its joy" (Prov. 14:10).

The most important step we can take, when the throb of loneliness pounds relentlessly in our hearts, is this third one toward God. For only He can heal the broken heart that even time fails to mend. The step to God is the most important one, because God is always near. We are never alone.

4

When Life Loses Its Flavor

One of my favorite things to do on my day off may seem a bit odd to most people. I like to do housework. Because my wife takes such good care of our home I don't get the chance to all the time, but when I do I thoroughly enjoy it!

My very favorite chore is vacuuming. I think that's because I like to see the newly made lines in our thick carpet. Since I'm allergic to dust, I've learned to be very meticulous about dusting. I also get a kick out of cleaning mirrors and scrubbing sinks. Bathroom floors I usually leave to my wife (I have bad knees) but laundry is another matter. As far as I'm concerned, the two of us aren't able to generate nearly enough dirty laundry to satisfy my craving to wash, dry, iron, and sort clothes.

But there is one domestic chore that I have never been able to learn. I can't cook. I have a hunch that I was born with an innate inability to cook an edible meal, because no one can cook as poorly as I can. Ask my ex-roommates. Ask my wife. Ask our neighbor's dog.

The problem is not that the food I cook is unhealthy. It isn't that I don't read the directions. The problem is that somehow I have developed the unfortunate ability of removing all flavor from whatever I cook.

Jesus said that salt which has lost its taste is no longer good for anything except to be thrown out and trodden under foot by men (Matt. 5:13). That is descriptive of my cooking. Whether steak, scrambled eggs, or chicken noodle soup, it all ends up tasting the same.

Just as I love to do housework, I love to be alive! I revel in meeting new people, studying in my office, relaxing in my recliner, going out on a date with my wife, silently watching a sunset, or writing a letter to old friends. But sometimes, life loses its taste for me. When that happens I feel a bit like blue jeans that have been washed too many times, and have lost their color and shape. And sometimes I feel about as useful as a bug on a windshield.

Boredom

One spring day, Ziggy slumped listlessly into his favorite over-stuffed beanbag chair to dream of life as it could be:

I could do so much more with my life. . . . I could become a public official . . . a leader of men . . . author legislation that would elevate mankind to heights untold . . . or I could become a great adventurer . . . sailing into uncharted seas with the salt spray in my face and the wind at my back . . . discovering new frontiers. There are so many things I could do with my life . . . if I could only get out of this chair (Tom Wilson, *The Ziggy Treasury*, Sheed, Andrews and McMeel, p. 106).

Like Ziggy, we have all been struck by the thought that somewhere out there life must have more to offer than what we've experienced so far. At times life loses its flavor for all of us. And when it does, the feeling that results is usually boredom.

Boredom is the feeling of being stuck in the groove on a record. It's the feeling of being all dried up, or of living on a treadmill. For a junior higher in the middle of summer vacation, boredom is having nothing to do. For others, like the warehouseman or the housewife, it means having to do the same thing over and over. For still others, it may mean an inability to appreciate the freedom and advantages they have.

Boredom has a paradoxical quality to it. It combines a certain degree of restlessness with a good deal of weariness and listlessness. The restlessness is to see something new, to taste something tangy, to try something different. Yet at the same time there is a sense that nothing really matters, that nothing would make any difference, that nothing is worth the energy anyway. Boredom is the drumming on the desk by an antsy executive, and the shrug of the shoulders by a weary waitress.

Particularly annoying is the fact that we can even be bored by things that give us great enjoyment. Racquetball is one of my favorite forms of exercise. But in weeks when I've been able to squeeze a number of matches into my schedule, I find something curious happening. I get bored. I can play only so much racquetball in a given week without losing interest in it.

No matter how much you enjoy your job, no matter how much variety you may have in your life, no matter how "perfect" your circumstances, at some time you lose interest in life. Sooner or later you find yourself feeling stuck, static, and stagnant.

For those of us who want to make the most of our lives, who want to experience and enjoy everything life has to offer, being bored is a particularly frustrating experience. It just doesn't seem fair that life can be so drab and tedious, when we want so very much for it to be colorful and tasty.

There Must Be More!

Close to 3,000 years ago an extremely wealthy and powerful king named Solomon found himself utterly bored with life. Listen to his description of existence in the opening chapter of the Book of Ecclesiastes:

"Vanity of vanities," says the Preacher,
"vanity of vanities! All is vanity . . .
A generation goes and a generation comes,
but the earth remains forever.

Also, the sun rises and the sun sets,
   and hastening to its place it rises there again.
Blowing toward the south
   then turning toward the north,
The wind continues swirling along;
   and on its circular courses the wind returns.
All the rivers flow into the sea,
   yet the sea is not full.
To the place where the rivers flow,
   there they flow again.
All things are wearisome;
   Man is not able to tell it.
The eye is not satisfied with seeing,
   Nor is the ear filled with hearing.
That which has been is that which will be,
   and that which has been done is that which will be
   done.
So there is nothing new under the sun" (Ecc. 1:2, 4-9).

Solomon was stuck. Life had lost its flavor for him. From his perspective life was one big merry-go-round, moving around and around in the same circle but never arriving anywhere.

Let's imagine that we are friends of Solomon and that he comes to us for advice on how to break out of his monotonous and mundane existence. What analysis might we make? What suggestions might we offer?

Perhaps we could say something like this: "Solomon, what you need is variety. Get out of your routine! Do something different! Make some new friends, visit some novel places, put some freshness and originality into your life."

Sounds like good advice, doesn't it? After all, it is a bit dull to do the same things day after day, see the same people, stare at the same walls, eat the same food, walk the same beat. Certainly there must be more to life than vanilla ice cream. Why not taste the other flavors too?

Solomon, being a man of means and influence, tried every

way possible to renew his interest in life, to discover something that could satisfy and appease his restlessness.

He tried the academic world of knowledge and wisdom: "I set my mind to seek and explore by wisdom concerning all that has been done under heaven. . . . I have magnified and increased wisdom, more than all who were over Jerusalem before me; and my mind has observed a wealth of wisdom and knowledge" (1:13, 16). He explored the world of entertainment and luxury: "I said to myself, 'Come now, I will test you with pleasure. So enjoy yourself'" (2:1). He experimented in the world of achievement: "I enlarged my works; I built houses for myself, I planted vineyards for myself; I made gardens and parks for myself . . . I made ponds of water for myself" (2:4-6). He probed the worlds of wealth and women: "I collected for myself silver and gold, and the treasures of kings and provinces. I provided for myself male and female singers and the pleasures of men—many concubines" (2:8). According to 1 Kings 11:3, Solomon had 700 wives and 300 concubines at his disposal. He couldn't complain about a lack of variety!

But was he satisfied? We would certainly think he should be! After all, he had fame, fortune, knowledge enough to author an encyclopedia, more women than he could manage, great achievements to his name, every pleasure known to man at his beck and call. Yet listen to Solomon's conclusion:

"All that my eyes desired I did not refuse them. I did not withhold my heart from any pleasure. . . . Thus I considered all my activities which my hands had done and the labor which I had exerted, and behold, all was vanity and striving after wind, and there was no profit under the sun" (2:10-11).

Wow! Everything a person could want right at his fingertips, and Solomon still wasn't satisfied! Remember the suggestion that boredom has a certain paradoxical quality to it? An ounce of restlessness to find something more, mixed with an ounce of weariness, the feeling that nothing really matters anyway? Sounds like Solomon—always looking for something different, something better, but in the end deciding that *nothing* really made any difference, that *nothing* was worth the effort!

But there is something more! The Psalmist David testified to it: "Thou wilt make known to me the path of life; in Thy presence is fullness of joy; in Thy right hand there are pleasures forever" (Ps. 16:11). Jesus assured His disciples of it: "I came that they might have life, and might have it abundantly . . . These things I have spoken to you, that My joy may be in you, and that your joy may be made full" (John 10:10; 15:11).

God has promised us an abundant and full life, not an empty one. He has promised us a meaningful and purposeful life, not a futile one. He has promised us an exciting and joyful life, not a boring one.

Boredom's Real Cause

Boredom's real cause is not a lack of variety. The malaise and frustration of boredom cannot be eradicated by accumulating more possessions, traveling to warmer climates, finding a new and better-looking spouse, earning another degree, or being offered a promotion.

The real cause of boredom is a lack of *meaning*. The real cause of boredom is a lack of *significance*. The real cause of boredom is a lack of *purpose*.

The problem we face in breaking out of a rut is not to find something different to do, but to discover the *meaning* and *purpose* of what we already are doing. For awhile we are able to cope with the tedium of repeating the same job day after day: cleaning the house, fixing the meals, ironing the clothes, weeding the garden, disciplining the kids, taking the car to the garage, paying the bills. But eventually something in us snaps and we stop in our tracks to ask: "*Why* am I doing these things? What is the point of all this?" When the job we do seems to have no purpose, we become bored. When our daily routine strikes us as meaningless, life loses its flavor.

Gail Sheehy describes the feelings of one kind of person

facing these questions, the career person whose primary motivation throughout life has been achievement. But then something snaps: "Whatever rung of achievement he has reached, the man of 40 usually feels stale, restless, burdened, and unappreciated. He worries about his health. He wonders, 'Is this all there is?'" (*Passages*, E.P. Dutton and Co., Inc., p. 45) When the answer to that question happens to be Yes, a person's zest for life and drive to achieve suddenly dissipate into discontent and apathy.

Both the Bible and secular psychology tell us that unless a person finds something or someone bigger than himself to commit his life to, his life will become meaningless and boring. What happens to so many of us, including committed Christians, is that we become *tranquilized by the trivial.* We get so caught up in merely making it through the routine of our day, in just doing all the items on our agenda, that we lose sight of any overall purpose. We forget why we are doing the things we are. We have become tranquilized by the trivial.

One question that I enjoy asking people I meet is, "What is your purpose in life? What gets you out of bed in the morning?" To my continual surprise, few people are able to even propose an answer to that question. Few of us are able to identify any orienting purpose to our lives. Consequently, we spend our lives pursuing things that are really trivial, that do not really matter in the long run.

Lloyd John Ogilvie described the attempt of one man to express his purpose in life:

Along with the other participants, he had been asked to doodle on a blank sheet of paper and draw a picture of his life as he saw it. He drew a pie with many lines through it representing the multiplicity of interests of his life. This man's honest drawing depicts the lives of most Christians. Many interests; no captivating, motivating, and unifying purpose. . . . Our families, jobs, friends, churches, involvements, and responsibilities pull us in a thousand directions, but there is nothing to pull us together in a consistent purpose which is expressed through all facets of our lives (*Loved and Forgiven,* Regal, pp. 44-45).

Daniel Levinson suggests that about every six to ten years adults encounter periods of stagnation, when a certain restlessness and weariness float to the surface of the conscious mind. And curiously, both those who fail to reach their goals and those who do reach them find within themselves the same sense of dissatisfaction that afflicted Solomon. That those of us who fail in our quests should be dissatisfied seems reasonable. But why should those who succeed be unhappy and bored? Levinson answers, "Often, a man who has accomplished his goals comes to feel trapped: his success is meaningless and he is now caught within a stultifying situation" (*The Seasons of a Man's Life,* Ballantine, p. 31). Even success, if it isn't ultimately meaningful, leaves a person with a feeling of futility and frustration. The cause of our boredom is a lack of meaning.

Breaking Out!

After being stirred by hearing Beethoven's passionate Ninth Symphony, Matthew Arnold despairingly remarked: "I am convinced that at the heart of the universe there is joy! But, oh, that I might find it!"

We all know deep inside that there is more to life than we have experienced so far, that the tedium and weariness and monotony that make up our routine is not the best that life has to offer us. We too are convinced that at the heart of the universe there is joy. But how do we find it? How do we break out of our insipid unsatisfying lives to experience life as it was meant to be lived? How do we break free of the frustration of boredom?

There are three steps we can take to break out of our boredom. They are not magical steps. They can't be done overnight. Growth does take place in spurts, but it never happens all at once! Yet following these steps will enable you to effectively defeat the doldrums.

● The first step toward breaking out of the blahs is to *be filled with the Holy Spirit*. The Apostle Paul instructed his readers with these words: "And do not get drunk with wine, for that is dissipation, but be filled with the Spirit" (Eph. 5:18).

Have you ever known an enthusiastic person who always seemed to be "up," who was passionately in love with life, who had the ability to squeeze the juices that flavor life out of almost every experience? Have you ever said to yourself, "I wish I could be like that"?

Do you want to know something? You can be like that! Enthusiasm is more than a boundless energy or a rose-colored naivete that only sees the rainbows and never the rain. The word *enthusiasm* comes from *en* meaning "in," and *theo* meaning "God." Enthusiasm is a result of being filled with God, of having your life controlled, directed, and empowered by the Holy Spirit.

According to Paul, Spirit-filled Christians are evidenced by . . . "speaking to one another in psalms and hymns and spiritual songs, singing and making melody" in their hearts "to the Lord; always giving thanks for all things in the name of our Lord Jesus Christ to God, even the Father" (Eph. 5:19-20).

That is the picture of an enthusiastic Christian, one who has a song in his heart and a spring in his step, who lives life with all of his being, who gives thanks for every circumstance instead of complaining about life's sour apples. The Spirit-filled Christian, the one who allows the Holy Spirit to direct and control each aspect of his life, will be able to live life enthusiastically.

● The second step in defeating the doldrums is to *change our attitude*. More important than the circumstances of our lives is our attitude. If we approach life with the attitude that life is humdrum, monotonous, and tasteless, then our lives are likely to be that way. But if we view life as something to celebrate, as something to be enjoyed and lived to the brim, then our days have the potential to be festive and delightful, whether our experiences are routine or not.

This truth was brought home to me one day while I was vegetating in front of the television watching reruns of the "Mary Tyler Moore Show." The character who awakened me to this profound truth was none other than the vacuous and bumbling Ted Baxter, anchorman at the news station where Mary was the associate producer. In this particular show, Mary was uncharacteristically despondent because her life seemed so routine and boring. In a moment of equally uncharacteristic brilliance, Ted analyzed her problem. Emphasizing each phrase with every ounce of dreariness he could muster, Ted said: "Here's your problem, Mary. Every day you get up, have breakfast, go to work, see your friends, go to lunch, work some more, drive home, fix dinner, read a book, watch TV, and go to bed."

As Ted droned tediously from phrase to phrase Mary became more and more depressed until her face drooped to the floor like the face of a 12-year-old bassett hound. "You know, Ted, you're right. I'm in a rut. I need to get out and do some new things, to make some changes."

"No, Mary, you've got it all wrong!" And then, raising his voice to a higher and more lively pitch with each phrase, Ted proposed, "What you need to do is to get up! Have breakfast! Go to work! See your friends! Go to lunch! Work some more! Drive home! Fix dinner! Read a book! Watch TV! Go to bed!" With emotion flooding his face and enthusiasm oozing from every syllable, Ted had sagely struck the right chord. More important than what we do is *how* we do it. Our attitude is the key: "Whatever you do, do your work heartily, as for the Lord rather than for men" (Col. 3:23).

One other comment on attitude and its relation to boredom deserves mention. Being bored is not all bad. Being bored is not a plague to be avoided at all costs. God can use our boredom to reveal things to us about ourselves and about life that we would never be able to hear while living in the fast lane.

In fact, many people have discovered that boredom and stagnation are essential to growth:

In every stage, developing is a process in which extremes are to some degree reconciled and integrated. Both generativity and its opposite pole, stagnation, are vital to a man's development. To become generative, a man must know how to stagnate . . ." (Levinson, *The Seasons of a Man's Life*, p. 30).

To reiterate, turning the frustration of boredom into fulfillment requires the proper attitude.

● But the most important step the victim of boredom can take is to *discover his purpose in living*. Albert Camus, the existentialist philosopher, opened his classic work *The Myth of Sisyphus* with this observation: "Judging whether or not life is worth living amounts to answering the fundamental question of philosophy" (Vintage Books, p. 3). That, indeed, is the question of the hour. Is life worth living? Does it have any significant purpose? Camus, Friedrich Nietzche, Sigmund Freud, Jean-Paul Sartre, Ernest Becker and a host of others resoundingly answered, "No! Life is an absurdity. There is no rhyme or reason to it. Life is irrational and without any ultimate significance."

The Christian loudly objects: "Life *does* have a purpose! It is meaningful!" But when pressed to the wall, are we able to express what that purpose is? Do we orient our lives around that purpose? Or have we become tranquilized by the trivial, so caught up in getting dinner on the table and the kids in bed that we never stop to think what our lives are all about?

The Apostle Paul never wavered in pursuit of his purpose. He knew exactly what made his life meaningful. In his farewell speech to close friends at Ephesus, he shared his life purpose: "But I do not consider my life of any account as dear to myself, in order that I may finish my course, and the ministry which I received from the Lord Jesus, to testify solemnly of the Gospel of the grace of God" (Acts 20:24). Paul knew what his life was all about, and he was able to express the purpose of his life in the same resolute manner in which he lived.

In the words of the Shorter Westminster Catechism, the

purpose of any human being is to "glorify God and to enjoy Him forever." Jesus told His disciples *how* they could glorify God: "By this is My Father glorified, that you bear much fruit, and so prove to be My disciples" (John 15:8).

To glorify God is to bear fruit. Just as the purpose of biological fruit is reproduction, so the purpose of spiritual fruit is reproduction. As Christians there are two kinds of spiritual fruit God calls for: the fruit of the Spirit in our lives—love, joy, peace, kindness, goodness, faithfulness, gentleness, and self-control (Gal. 5:22-23). And the fruit of ministry, by sharing God's good news with all those who do not know Him. To bear the fruit of the Spirit, and the fruit of ministry constitutes the purpose of our lives. Ted Engstrom and Edward Dayton help take us one step further in their book, *Strategy for Living,* where they tell us that we need to set specific, measurable goals to give substance to our purpose.

When it comes to *action*, too often we are content to leave words like "purposes" and "goals" in some foggy, undefined area. We talk about the grand purpose we have to "give glory to God," "to go into all the world," "to lead God-honoring lives." Good. These are words and phrases we need in our everyday language as Christians. But they can so easily become passwords by which we identify one another, rather than statements of what we intend to do (Regal, pp. 47-48).

When we realize that our purpose in life is to glorify God and to enjoy Him forever, we have taken a big step toward breaking out of boredom. But setting a goal of glorifying God by sharing the Gospel with our next door neighbor or by becoming a nurse's aide—this is what takes us out of the door. Nothing is as motivating as a well-chosen, measurable, accomplishable goal. Goals are what get the armchair quarterback out on the field.

What is our purpose? To glorify God and to enjoy Him forever! Not only are we to glorify God, we are to enjoy Him. Life is meant to be fun! We could perhaps learn an important lesson from a friar in a Nebraska monastery who late in life wrote:

> If I had my life to live over again,
> I'd try to make more mistakes next time.
>
> I would relax, I would limber up, I would be sillier than I have been on this trip.
>
> I know of very few things I would take seriously. I would take more trips. I would be crazier. I would climb more mountains, swim more rivers, and watch more sunsets.
>
> I would do more walking and looking.
>
> I would eat more ice cream and less beans (Thomas V. Bonoma and Dennis P. Slevin, *Executive Survival Manual*, CBI Publishing Co., pp. 58-59).

Glorify God, enjoy Him and His goodness, and life's flavor and fullness will be yours. May your life be the abundant one God promises it can be!

5

The Future Is Now

Columnist Robert T. Smith of the Minneapolis *Tribune* related to his readers a lesson he learned as his son's third birthday approached. Mark was a precocious and stubborn youngster who decided as plans for his third birthday party were being formulated that he didn't want to be three yet. Robert T. Smith patiently explained to Mark that he really didn't have any choice in the matter, because the laws of nature dictated that on this particular date he would become three. With all the authority of a General Patton, Mark announced, "But I'm not done being two yet." Being confronted with such superior logic, Robert T. Smith acquiesced to his son's desire, canceled the birthday party, and told Mark he could be two as long as he wanted.

Many of us have felt as Mark did. The calendar tells us it is time to graduate, to add a year to our age, or to celebrate another anniversary. Yet something inside tells us it isn't time. We aren't ready for college—why, we aren't done with high school yet! We aren't ready for marriage—we haven't finished with the single life. We aren't ready for middle age—we still want to be young. We aren't ready for retirement—we aren't done working. But whether we're ready or not, the future is now. Birthdays, holidays, anniversaries, and graduations sneak up on us and rudely announce that our future has arrived.

For Ethel Barrett the arrival of the future was announced by two of her grandsons. Mike and Sean found themselves in disagreement one day as the two youngsters picnicked on the beach. Sean contended that Grandmother Barrett was getting quite old while Mike staunchly defended her youthfulness. Finally, Sean delivered the clinching argument: "If Grandmother is not getting old, then how come the muscles in her arms are hanging down on the wrong side?"

Despite the stiff resistance from joggers, dieters, and health food experts, the future catches up with us all. Eventually the muscles in all of our arms will be hanging down on the wrong side, and that won't be the worst of the changes.

While some resent the invasion of the future into the present, others yearn to unlock its secrets. Millions of people invest money and energy in consulting astrologers and occultists hoping they just might be able to divulge the future. Yet there is something all of us are able to predict about the future—it will be different from the present. Alvin Toffler's primary thesis in his bestseller *Future Shock* is that the most difficult problem for Americans in the future will be coping with change. Change is inevitable, and the rate at which things are changing is accelerating all the time.

Within each of us is a desire to be able to face the future fearlessly. We don't want to spend each night worrying about what is going to happen tomorrow, and whether we will be able to adapt to its changes. We want to be at peace with the past, present, and future. We want to feel confident, secure, even eager to face the challenges of a new day.

But for many of us, our desire to face the future fearlessly is frustrated by anxiety. Like a parasite invading the tissues of our lives, anxiety feeds on every hint of change that pops into our future. Worry, fear, and dread become our bedpartners. Instead of eagerly anticipating the opportunities and challenges of the future, we find ourselves cowering in intimidation—petrified, paralyzed, powerless to proceed. We aren't always sure why we feel anxious, or just what it is about the future that is so frightening. And this uncertainty only makes the feeling that much more frustrating.

In examining my own attitudes toward the future and in talking with other people about their feelings, I have concluded that there are four approaches toward the future. Three of them heighten our sense of frustration and turn out to be more crippling than constructive. They serve to deprive us of our enjoyment of life and to rob us of the experience of fullness that God desires for us. The fourth approach is the healthiest and most biblical and is the way out of the frustration of fear. This is the attitude God instructs us to take in order to defeat our dread and to axe anxiety out of our lives. Let's examine each of the approaches toward the future.

Fear of the Future

The first approach turns out to be the very frustration that we are trying to conquer. Yet it is probably the most common attitude toward the future. It is fear, a gnawing apprehension about what troubles might move in when we open the door to tomorrow. The most common way to approach the future is to *worry* about it.

We worry about what it's going to be like to live away from home for the first time, about whether we'll ever make new friends as good as the ones we've grown up with. We worry about whether we'll *ever* get married. We worry about paying the bills. We worry about when our first child will walk. We worry about losing our eyesight or our hearing or our memory.

As we grow up we learn to be very creative in our worrying about the future. We are able to imagine all sorts of awful things that might happen to us or our children. As a society that has been raised on Murphy's Law, we have come to believe that anything that possibly can go wrong will go wrong. We've even learned corollaries to Murphy's Law that tell us,

"Nothing is as easy as it looks," "Everything takes twice as long as you've planned," and "The shortest route between two points is always closed for repairs."

Fear and anxiety are extremely painful, and incredibly difficult to shake. The popular playwright Tennessee Williams once confessed:

Whether or not we admit it to ourselves, we are all haunted by a truly awful sense of impermanence. I have always had a particularly keen sense of this at New York cocktail parties, and perhaps that is why I drink martinis almost as fast as I can snatch them from the tray. . . . . Fear and evasion are the two little beasts that chase each other's tails in the revolving wine cage of our nervous world (Quoted by Vernon Grounds in *Emotional Problems and the Gospel,* Zondervan, p. 20)..

Because the future is so unreliable, it is natural for us to be somewhat fearful of it. We all value a certain degree of security, of sameness to our lives. We value having a steady job, dependable relationships, and at least the semblance of an orderly routine. But the future can't promise us security and stability. Getting a hold on the future can be as elusive and slippery as stopping a car in an icy intersection.

David Koop, son of the world-famous pediatric surgeon, C. Everett Koop, had plans for his future. At 20 years of age this adventurous and brilliant Christian seemed to have a full and exciting life just waiting for him. But the future proved to be especially treacherous for David Koop. While mountain climbing in New Jersey, he stumbled and plunged to his death. The future offers us no guarantees.

Perhaps the most frightening aspect of the future is the one certain event that waits patiently for us all—death. In his Pulitzer Prize winning book, *The Denial of Death,* Ernest Becker suggests that the fear of death is the prime motivating factor of all that we do:

"The prospect of death," Dr. Johnson said, "wonderfully concentrates the mind." The main thesis of this book is that it does much more than that: the idea of death, the fear of it, haunts the human animal like nothing else; it is a mainspring of human activity—activity designed largely to avoid the fatality of death, to overcome it by denying in some way that it is the final destiny for man (The Free Press, p. ix).

Whether it is the prospect of death, the dread of failure, or just the uncertainty of things to come, the future can be overwhelmingly frightening. Abraham, the great patriarch, felt this fear. In Hebrews 11:8 we read, "By faith Abraham, when he was called, obeyed by going out to a place which he was to receive for an inheritance; and he went out, not knowing where he was going." Abraham had no idea of what the future held for him when God called him to leave his home and venture out into an unknown land. For Abraham, as for many of us, the future was a source of uncertainty and fear.

Apathy Toward the Future—Attachment to the Past

Some people find themselves apathetic toward the future because they are anchored to the past. If the future is uncertain and frightening, at least the past is safe. That is a place they have already been, a territory they have already explored. Because the past is so secure, so safe, they are content to spend their lives living in days gone by, instead of venturing out into the precarious prospects of the future. They become anchored to the past, shackled by their memories.

Sometimes we are anchored by past failures. We can't forget the business setback we suffered, the broken relationships, or the time we failed to score in an important game. The humiliation of forgetting the words to the song in front of an auditorium full of people is burned into our memory. Everytime we think of our failure, the hurt and anguish well up inside of us and we vow never again to put ourselves into another situation where we might have our failure publicly displayed.

So many people never experience God's best for them. They skulk under limits self-imposed solely because of their fear that they might fail again. Everyone has failed at some time; many people have failed so often they've become quite proficient at it. Consider this example:

A young man ran for the legislature in Illinois, and was badly swamped.

He next entered business, failed, and spent 17 years of his life paying up the debts of a worthless partner.

He was in love with a beautiful woman to whom he became engaged; then she died.

Reentering politics, he ran for Congress, and was badly defeated.

He then tried to get an appointment to the United States Land Office, but failed.

He became a candidate for the United States Senate, and was badly defeated.

Two years later he was again defeated (Quoted by George Bowman in *How to Succeed with Your Money*, Moody Press, p. 145).

If ever a man had a reason to quit, to retreat into the past and blend into the background, it was this man. But Abraham Lincoln wouldn't quit. He wouldn't let his past failures prevent him from trying again. He shrugged off the chains of the past and went on to lead thousands of destitute slaves into the freedom they had yearned after for so long.

While some are anchored to the past by personal failure, others are anchored to the past by personal loss. The grief of losing a spouse to cancer or a son to war can often so possess a person that he is unable to continue living a productive and full life. No matter how sunny and bright the future may be, the person engulfed by grief can see only the darkness and the agony of the past.

A favorite thespian haunt of university locals in Minneapolis is Dudley Riggs Brave New Workshop. One of the plays done there included an act with two elderly women tottering around a kitchen complaining to each other about all the bad habits their husbands had. The one woman claimed that her husband would never shut the cupboards when he took the dishes out and that he always left the freezer door open when he snuck some ice cream. To emphasize her point she shuffled over to the freezer where sure enough, the freezer door was ajar and the food had begun to melt. The other woman complained just as loudly that her husband smoked incessantly and smelled up all his clothes. Why, even now she was running a load of wash to get the smoke out of his good clothes.

But as the play progressed, the audience became aware that the husbands of the women were dead, and had been for some time. Yet those two old women went on living and complaining as though nothing had changed. Their means of coping with grief was to pretend that the tragedy had never happened.

While some people are anchored by failure or grief, others are anchored to the past by their successes. How good it feels to relive the trophies we won in school, the good times we had with our families, the speeches that everyone praised! Why go on into the future when the past has been so rewarding? Barbra Streisand's song "The Way We Were" expresses a truth we all know, that "what's too painful to remember, we simply choose to forget." The hours of hard work fade into the air and what comes to mind are the triumphs, the victories, the successes. If only we could turn back the clock and live that day, week or year over again—that would be our heaven!

Certain memories *are* to be cherished. I count as some of my most precious possessions the memories I have of winning the regional basketball championship, of canoeing the crystal clear lakes of southern Canada, of honeymooning in Hawaii. But memories can also be chains that prevent us from taking risks now, from meeting new people and exploring untapped resources. When we allow ourselves to be anchored to the past we become mired in our memories. We become like scratched records that play the same note over and over again.

When we allow memories to keep us from living life now, they can become a trap to escape from instead of treasures to be cherished. As much as we'd like to stop the clock and camp where we are, God keeps beckoning us onward as He beckoned Abraham, calling us to pack up our tents and go forward to possess a land we've never seen.

The Fantasy of the Future

The third attitude toward the future is to think that tomorrow holds the happiness that escaped you today. Perhaps this last year hasn't been an especially happy or successful one. Maybe a relationship you valued went sour or a project you poured your life into never turned out.

When we feel ourselves tainted by disappointment or discontent, the temptation is to assure ourselves that tomorrow will be better. Success, love, happiness, freedom, prosperity—all await us tomorrow.

It is important that we recognize the difference between *faith* and *fantasy*. In Hebrews 11:1, we read, "Now faith is the assurance of things hoped for, the conviction of things not seen." It is healthy to fix our hopes on what God has promised us will happen. It is healthy to dream big dreams, to make plans and set goals. It is quite true that goals are statements of faith about the future, motivating us to accomplish more than we would otherwise. It is also true that the Bible commands us to be eagerly looking to the future for the return of Christ. To dream, to hope, to set goals—all these are expressions of faith that should be valued and cherished.

But to fantasize about the future is debilitating. While dreaming dreams, hoping for what God has promised, and setting goals give us strength and motivation to live more energetically and effectively in the present, fantasizing tends to anesthetize us. Fantasy blocks any constructive action. It is like being locked in neutral. We grit our teeth so that we can endure today while waiting for our ship to dock at "Candy Land" or "Fantasy Island."

To assume that tomorrow will bring nirvana to our restless souls, and a banquet of delights to our hungry senses, is to live in a prison of perpetual discontent. The reality of time is that tomorrow never comes. Life is always today. The person who spends his time waiting for the future and fantasizing about its happiness won't even notice when the joys that struggled to flower today wilt underneath his feet.

The Future as an Adventure in Faith

So far we have seen that the approaches many people take toward the future fail to alleviate the frustration of anxiety. To fantasize about the future does remove the feeling of fear, but only by distorting what the future really offers. Fantasy means living in a world of illusions and fairy tales. Because of its unreality, we must reject fantasy as an adequate means to deal with our fears.

To hide our heads in the sands of the past is futile, for it distorts the reality of what the past was, as well as what the future may be.

But there is an alternative—to approach the future as an *adventure in faith.* Faith is the antidote to fear. To be free from our fear of the future, we need to approach the future as an adventure in faith.

For Abraham and Moses, for David, Isaiah, and Paul, and all the other great heroes of the Bible, life was an adventure in faith. The faith chapter, Hebrews 11, lists examples of men and women who were called by God to leave behind a secure and stable life and to launch out into an adventure of faith. They are people who changed the world, and whom the Bible lauds as great heroes.

● The distinguishing feature of these great biblical heroes was their attitude toward the future. First of all, they approached the future with *faith.* They had faith that even though they didn't know where they were going, God did. They weren't afraid of the future because they had faith that God would lead them to the right country, to the right people, to the right decisions, to the right career, to the right mate. They had confidence that God would care for them when they were victims of accidents, or when their bodies got old and sick. Because of their confidence that God was in control, they didn't waste their energy fretting about the future.

Dr. Wilhelm De Nejs and his wife lived in Indonesia, where they worked with sufferers from eye disease. Being partially blind himself, Dr. De Nejs was highly motivated to use his gifts to help others with the same kind of problem. But when a new government took control, Dr. De Nejs and his wife were forced to leave their work. They made plans to drive their old car from Indonesia to the Netherlands where their five children were living. Their Indonesian friends gathered enough money to ship their car to Singapore.

But the only resource this couple had to get them from Singapore to the Netherlands was faith. They had little money for food or gas. There were no detailed maps to direct them through Pakistan, India, Afghanistan, Iran, Iraq, and the many other countries they needed to cross. There were very few roads. They drove through a wicked sandstorm that left a trail of dead camels in its wake. They traveled for two weeks through a desert without any drinking water for themselves, surviving only by drinking the water from their car's radiator. They waded their car across rivers. They survived an accident in Yugoslovia. Finally, after six months, having crossed 20,000 miles of deserts, jungles, rivers, and mountains, they arrived in the Netherlands where they were greeted by their five ecstatic children (Robert Schuller, *Move Ahead with Possibility Thinking,* Revell, pp. 159-164).

To face the future demands faith. We have no idea of what lies ahead for our lives, what mountains we will be forced to cross, what rivers we'll have to wade through, what seemingly impossible situations will confront us. But as Christians, we can know that God will see us through every circumstance, that He will provide for our every need. God assures us:

Do not fear, for I have redeemed you; I have called you by name; you are Mine! When you pass through the waters, I will be with you; and through the rivers, they will not overflow you. When you walk through fire, you will not be scorched, nor will the flame burn you. For I am the Lord your God (Isa. 43:1-3).

Because our God loves us, because we are precious to Him, and because He holds our future in His hand, we can approach the future without fear. We can stride confidently into tomorrow, knowing that our God has promised us strength and wisdom for every situation we might encounter. We can face the future in faith.

● The great heroes of the Bible approached the future as an *adventure.* Notice what is said about them in Hebrews 11:8-9, and 13:

By faith Abraham, when he was called, obeyed by going out to a place which he was to receive for an inheritance; and he went out, not knowing where he was going. By faith he lived as an alien in the land of promise, as in a foreign land, dwelling in tents with Isaac and Jacob. . . . . All these died in faith, without receiving the promises, but having seen them and having welcomed them from a distance, and having confessed that they were strangers and exiles on the earth.

These great people of faith lived out their earthly existence as exiles, as people in transit. God had called them to leave their past behind, to give up their security, and to venture out in search of a land of abundance and peace and prosperity. But they never found that land. They spent their whole lives as pioneers, as aliens and exiles in a strange land. The dictionary defines adventure as "an exciting and dangerous undertaking," "an unusual, stirring, often romantic experience," as a "risk." The patriarchs of the Christian faith didn't have much of a choice—their lives were going to be adventurous whether they wanted them to be or not! Always looking, always on the move, always in transit, and never at home.

Like the patriarchs of Hebrews 11, we are people in transit. The Bible makes it clear that "this earth is not our home, we're only passing through." The patriarchs learned finally that the land they were looking for wasn't on earth but in heaven. "But as it is, they desire a better country, that is a heavenly one. Therefore God is not ashamed to be called their God; for He has prepared a city for them" (Heb. 11:16).

The Christian is not a settler but a pioneer. As Christians we are called to live a life of adventure, a life of newness and freshness and vitality. The adventurer is never quite content with where he is or what he has experienced. He realizes that God always has something more for him—more people to meet, more truth to grasp, more experiences to own. The Christian adventurer is always a bit restless to experience more of God's fullness and power, a restlessness that will not be satisfied until heaven becomes his home. Like the patriarchs, the Christian adventurer senses God continually calling him to move on, to leap out into the unknown in faith, to leave behind the failures, fears, and memories of the past.

Because so many of us have never seen our own lives as adventurous, we choose to feed on the adventures of other people. We park in front of our televisions to be titillated and thrilled by soap operas, beauty pageants, sporting events, and detective stories. The adventure, success, and excitement of the TV characters become our own as we live our lives through them. How can our lives be adventurous when we are trapped by the routines and responsibilities of day-to-day life? If only we could be like Superwoman or Hans Solo and Luke Skywalker—that would be adventure!

When we content ourselves to feed like leeches on the adventures of talk-show guests we miss what God has for us. Each day can be an adventure if we will let it, because our God is a God of newness! He doesn't want us to be content living on experiences of yesterday. He wants to do something new in us every day. Through the Prophet Isaiah, God explained to His people that while it was great to remember that

He was the one who delivered Israel out of Egypt centuries before, He was more concerned that they experience the new thing He had for them now: "Do not call to mind the former things, or ponder things of the past. Behold, I will do something new, *now* it will spring forth; will you not be aware of it?" (Isa. 43:18-19)

God wants to do new things in our lives every day, yet we are so often blind to them. God doesn't want us to live on our relationship with Him of 20 years ago. He doesn't want us to have to think back to years gone by to share the last time God answered one of our prayers. He wants our relationship with Him to be as fresh as a new snowfall and as up to date as today's calendar. Life can be an adventure for us, if we will only open our eyes to the new things God has for us each day, and have the faith to believe that there is more to life than what we've already experienced.

● The patriarchs recognized that the *future is now*. They did not allow themselves to vegetate in their fantasies. If they had decided to wait until they reached the land God promised them to enjoy their lives or to accomplish anything, they would have waited forever. They never did reach that land. They never did see their dreams fulfilled. But that didn't prevent them from living adventurously and abundantly, or from changing their world.

God has one message for those of us who are waiting until we reach Fantasy Island before we get on with the business of life—don't wait! Don't wait to enjoy life. Whatever situation you are in, there is something to enjoy. David prayed, "Thou wilt make known to me the path of life; in Thy presence is fullness of joy; in Thy right hand there are pleasures forever" (Ps. 16:11). Jesus has promised us an abundant life *now*. We don't need to wait until we're better educated, married, richer, or until we've traveled more, to experience the abundant life God has promised.

Neither do we need to wait until tomorrow to change our world. In one church I was a part of, we had a nursery school to which many non-Christian parents sent their kids. After having their children in the school a few weeks, those parents would come and plead with us to call off their kids! They told us their little three- and four-year-olds were driving them crazy singing "Jesus loves me" and making them say "thank you" to Jesus at every meal. Those three-year-olds were changing their worlds! They didn't wait for seminary to start sharing their faith. In their innocence they simply shared with their parents what God had taught them that day.

We can begin changing our world today. We already have the gifts and the power we need to make an impact. We don't need to wait until tomorrow to share what God has done for us today.

The future can be an adventure in faith for each of us. We don't need to be afraid of what the future might bring. We don't need to be anchored to the past by our failures, our grief, or our successes. We don't need to become victims of our fantasies. Because our God is a God of love, of newness, and of power, we can approach each day with the confidence and faith that today will be the most exciting and adventurous day of our lives. Don't wait until tomorrow—the future is now!

6

Who Wants To Kiss a Frog?

Once upon a time there was a frog.
But he wasn't *really* a frog.
He was a prince who looked and felt like a frog.
A wicked witch had cast a spell on him,
and only the kiss of a beautiful maiden could save him.
But no one wanted to kiss this frog!
So there he sat—an unkissed prince in frog form.
But one day along came a beautiful maiden
who gave this frog a great big smack.
Crash—Boom—ZAP!
There he was, a handsome, dashing prince.
And you know the rest—they lived happily ever after.
   (Serendipity House, Colorado Springs)

The story of the frog who was really a prince is one we heard
many times as we grew up. Like most fairy tales it ends happily
when the beautiful princess kisses the ugly frog and he is
transformed by this simple but profound act of love back into
the charming prince. The point of the story is equally familiar.
In one sense, each person is an ugly frog waiting to be kissed,
waiting to be loved and accepted, and to be transformed by
that love into a charming prince or princess.

But what about those of us who are still waiting to be kissed? After all, who wants to kiss a frog? For one reason or another we all know what rejection feels like. We've been rejected by universities, by companies, by social groups, by friends, by sweethearts, and even by family members. We've been rejected because of nationality, weight, skin color, income level, IQ, religion, or for no reason at all. Sometimes we may feel rejected without really having been so. Whether the rejection is real or imagined, the pain we feel can be as tormenting and destructive as cancer. It is, in the words of Ernest Campbell, "the hardest blow of all" (*Locked in a Room with Open Doors,* Word, p. 12).

Risking Rejection

It was St. Valentine's Day, the day when timid lovers grow bold and confess the longing and affection that has been secretly nurtured in their hearts for so long. Charlie Brown eagerly danced from one tree to another, his heart racing as he anxiously spied the landscape to insure that his mission would not be discovered by any passersby. Bright-eyed and grinning he made a final dash to the front door where he slipped a large heart-shaped valentine through the mail slot. With a smile of satisfaction he turned to sneak back home, but was stopped short by the sound of the mail slot clanking.

Looking back he saw that his valentine had been tossed back out with a note paper-clipped to it. Forlornly his sad eyes read this note: "Dear contributor, Thank you for submitting your valentine. We regret to inform you that it does not suit our present needs."

Taking a risk can be frightening. Calling a girl to ask her out on a first date, interviewing for a job, investing in a new business deal, or proposing marriage—these are almost always traumatic, because they involve the risk of being rejected. Mailing that valentine was certainly a courageous act for Charlie Brown, especially considering his track record. He took a risk, hoping to get kissed. But when the dust had settled, poor Charlie Brown still smelled like a frog.

One of the strongest desires resonating in our hearts is to be accepted, to be valued for who we are, just as we are. We want to be loved. We want people to realize that we have something to offer, that we have our own beauty, that we are special.

But more often than seems fair, that desire is frustrated by rejection. Instead of finding open arms and an affirming smile, we find ourselves banished, exiled from love like Romeo exiled from the kingdom of Verona. And we sit in our swamp, wet, smelly, and feeling very much like frogs, waiting for our prince or princess.

Have you ever felt like a frog, like a discarded dishrag, or an unwanted age spot? Have you ever been rejected by someone you deeply cared about, whose love and respect you wanted more than anything? Maybe it was a boyfriend or a girlfriend, a son or daughter. Maybe it was a parent, coach, an employer, or a close friend. If you have, you know how painful rejection can be.

Early in my seminary career, I met a petite, bubbly, attractive young teacher. Mustering up all my charm, I boldly asked her out, and within a short while we were dating regularly. About nine months into the relationship I became convinced that this was the girl God wanted me to marry. I knew she must be the one because every time I thought about her I would get goose bumps, start to perspire, and begin to salivate. What more evidence does a person need?

I lay awake nights planning just the right way to propose. Being in seminary I finally decided to use a proposal with a catchy introduction, a concise propositional statement, three main points with ample illustrations, and to conclude by giving an invitation!

At last the day I had planned for arrived. It was a gorgeous spring day. The buds on the trees were popping out of their winter cocoons and the green in the grass was beginning to awaken from its long hiberation. We drove to a nearby lake for a brisk walk and a chance to smell the crisp, clean air and enjoy the warm sunshine.

Then, with my heart pounding like a sledgehammer, I began my well-rehearsed proposal. I moved smoothly through my catchy introduction, the concise propositional statement, the three amply illustrated points, and closed with the traditional call to commitment: "Will you marry me?"

There was silence. I quickly sensed that my "sermon" had not evoked the response I intended. Later I chastized myself for not bringing a tape-recording of "Just as I Am" to set the proper mood for the invitation.

Slowly she began her reply. She assured me that she cared for me, that I was a good person, and that she respected me. It was one of those speeches that I knew couldn't end with anything other than "But I don't want to marry you." Knowing what was coming I steeled myself for the final blow. But despite my bravest efforts, I felt completely and hopelessly crushed when her answer finally came.

Despair slapped me like ice water tossed in my face. The numbness and the shock turned to pain worse than I'd ever felt before, and as I watched her walk away, I reluctantly gave in to the tears that had for some time begged to be released.

Though I sensed even then that what she had done was for our best and that she really did care for me, I couldn't help but feel like a fat, ugly, smelly frog. Rejection is the hardest blow of all.

One morning a girl at the Minneapolis emergency phone center received a call that was quite unlike any other she had ever gotten. The only sound from the other end of the line was the grunting of a person she quickly sensed was in desperate need of help. She frantically attempted to figure out a method of communicating with the caller, until she ingeniously asked him if he might be able to tap out his address with his fingers. After three long, tense hours the girl managed to decipher his address and dispatch the rescue squad to his apartment. When the rescue squad arrived they discovered why the man was unable to talk. He had placed a gun under his chin, and with a pull of the trigger had blown his face off. They also found a note explaining why he had done such a drastic thing. His fiancee had left him for someone else.

Rejection cuts. It angers. It tears and eats at us and makes us want to strike back, to lash out. Sometimes we do strike back. Other times we bury the pain inside of us, allowing it to fester in our gut like an ulcer, flaring up at every hint of the old wound.

How do you handle the frustration of being rejected? For as sure as you have been stung with rejection before, you will also be stung with it again. Not everyone you meet is going to think you are as wonderful as your mother tells people you are. And despite your most earnest efforts to be friendly, to do your job well, to get along with people and be liked, there will still be those who will thumb their noses at you. Unfortunately, there is no vaccine for rejection. It hurts every time.

Somebody Loves Me

Yet as painful as rejection can be, there is good news! It is possible, through the power of God, to be rejected and to live joyfully anyway. God does have a kiss left for the rejected frog. For those of us stuck in the swamp of rejection, the Gospel of Jesus Christ offers hope of healing, acceptance, and love.

Rejection still hurts, but it's easier to take when we know that at least one person loves us. If someone reacts very negatively to one of my sermons and loudly criticizes me, I quite naturally feel hurt. Yet I am not overwhelmed by their criticism because I know that my wife still loves me and will give me her support.

The message of the Gospel is that at least one Person will always love me. One Person loves me so much that He died for me. One Person has said that His love for me won't be squelched by anything—not by death, trials, famine, or failure. The message of the Gospel is that God loves me.

A number of years ago a drawbridge operator named Gus invited his ten-year-old son Peter to spend the day with him at the bridge. Peter was delighted! He had always been proud of his father, and he was excited that he would be able to help his dad control the large, imposing bridge. Wait till his friends heard about this!

When they reached the bridge Gus showed his son how the levers for the bridge worked. An old fishing boat was easing up the river, so Gus and Peter set the drawbridge in motion. With a grinding hum and a few creaks, the huge gears lifted the bridge skyward, and the boat passed under it and on up the river.

While the boat crept up the meandering river Gus checked his gauges and jotted notes in his report book. Suddenly the serenity of that morning was shattered by a loud, familiar sound. It was the piercing whistle of the 10:05 southbound train.

The 10:05 was a little early—and a little late in blowing the warning whistle. Gus knew that he must lower the bridge quickly to avoid a tragedy.

Gus's big gloved hands grasped the shiny levers and pulled. He looked over his shoulder for Peter. Where was the boy? "Peter!" Gus's stomach knotted as his eyes nervously darted up and down the bridge. "Peter!"

The bridge began its descent. "Daddy! Daddy!" Frantic with worry, Gus peered over the edge and saw his son atop the huge bridge gears. The giant teeth of the rotating machinery had consumed the boy's jacket. Now his hand and arm were being devoured, slowly pulling his entire body in the grinding gears.

Gus reached for the levers. But here came the 10:05 loaded with passengers, whistle howling, roaring toward the bridge. "Daddy, help me!" The terror of the boy's voice seemed to pound with every muscle of his father's body.

Gus glanced at the train, then at his helpless son. In that split second, Gus was faced with deciding between the life of his pleading son, or the hundreds of lives aboard the rushing train.

Gus held firm on the levers. The bridge continued its bow of mercy for the passengers aboard the train.

Gus wept as the machinery squeezed the life from his only son. As the boy's shrieks melted into echoes, the 10:05 sped across the old bridge. The vacationing passengers had no idea what had just transpired below the bridge. In air-conditioned comfort, they waved and smiled at Gus as they whizzed past.

("The Bridge: A Haunting Story of Love," *Group* Magazine, March/April 1980, pp. 22-23).

God loves us. He loves us so much that He sent His only Son, Jesus Christ, to be rejected and crucified so that we might have life now and forever. We are so important, so precious, so valuable, that God allowed His only Son to be crushed by the mob in Jerusalem so that we might be able to be forgiven and accepted. There is no one in the world more important to God than you, and He has proved that by not even sparing the life of His Son. You are loved by God.

Have you been rejected? Have you been abandoned or deserted, scorned or insulted? Are you a frog still waiting to be kissed? Do you ache inside from the humiliation of sitting in the swamp alone for so long?

There is good news for you! Even though everyone else may have left you, even though you may feel that no one cares, the message of the Gospel is that somebody loves you! Somebody loves you enough to die for you. Somebody has bent down into the swamp and kissed your slimy, wart-covered forehead and has transformed you into a handsome prince or a beautiful princess. You are loved, you are accepted, you are special, you belong!

Somebody Understands Me!

To the person who has been rejected, the faithful love of even one person can be a great comfort. Yet we humans have a quirk about us that takes comfort for our hurt in knowing that someone else hurts too. The old proverb "Misery loves company" has been ratified by all of us over and over again. We like to know that we aren't the only ones who have ever been turned down for a job, who have dropped a pass in the end zone, whose girlfriend or wife has left for another. In fact, the person best able to comfort us is the one who has experienced the same kind of failure or rejection or hurt that we have. Their comfort is more meaningful to us because we know that they understand what we're going through.

That's why the Gospel is such good news for those of us who have felt rejected. Not only are we loved by someone important, but we're loved by someone who understands. God understands our hurt because He was rejected! God became a man in the person of Jesus Christ. Jesus felt pain. He knew what it was to work hard, to get up early, to be hungry, to lose a close friend to death, to cry, and to ache. The author of the Book of Hebrews tells us of Jesus: "Therefore, He had to be made like His brethren in all things. . . . For since He Himself was tempted in that which He has suffered, He is able to come to the aid of those who are tempted" (Heb. 2:17-18). God understands our hurt because in Jesus Christ He experienced suffering, temptation—and rejection.

No chapter in the Bible more poignantly describes the pain that Christ experienced than Isaiah 53. Written centuries before the life of Jesus Christ, it prophetically portrays His rejection, His suffering, and the punishment He endured so that we might have a new quality of life.

> He had no dignity or beauty
> > to make us take notice of Him.
> There was nothing attractive about Him,
> > nothing that would draw us to Him.
> We despised Him and rejected Him;
> > He endured suffering and pain.
> No one would even look at Him—
> > we ignored Him as if He were nothing.

But He endured the suffering
   that should have been ours,
   the pain that we should have borne.
All the while we thought that His suffering
   was punishment sent by God.
But because of our sins He was wounded,
   beaten because of the evil we did.
We are healed by the punishment He suffered,
   made whole by the blows He received. . . .
He was arrested and sentenced and led off to die,
   and no one cared about His fate. . . .
The Lord says,
"It was My will that He should suffer;
His death was a sacrifice to bring forgiveness. . . .
After a life of suffering He will again have joy;
He will know that He did not suffer in vain. . . .
And so I will give Him a place of honor,
   a place among great and powerful men.
He willingly gave His life
   and shared the fate of evil men.
He took the place of many sinners,
   and prayed that they might be forgiven"
                  (Isa. 53:2-5, 8, 10-12, GNB).

Because God became a man, He understands what it feels like to be rejected. He knows what it is to be scoffed at, to feel unattractive, to be misunderstood, to be unfairly abused. We are loved by someone who has been there, who is able to comfort us because He's felt the same hurt. God knows what it feels like to be a frog. He spent 33 years in the swamp.

Somebody Can Heal Me!

But there is more good news. Not only are we loved and understood, but we can be healed! God cures our bruises and wounds and remakes our broken lives. As Isaiah describes the rejection and agony of God in Jesus Christ, he gives promise of our healing: "We are healed by the punishment He suffered, made whole by the blows He received."

Our shattered lives can be remade! We can have a new beginning, a new confidence, a new power to live! We can be whole again. But how? The answer to that question comes from the life of the lonely Prophet Jeremiah.

One day God told Jeremiah to go to the potter's house because He had something to show him. Jeremiah did what he was told, and this was his report:

The vessel he was making of clay was spoiled in the hand of the potter; so he remade it into another vessel, as it pleased the potter to make. Then the word of the Lord came to me, saying, "Can I not, O house of Israel, deal with you as this potter does?" declares the Lord. "Behold, like the clay in the potter's hand, so are you in My hand" (Jer. 18:4-5)

Like the potter remaking a spoiled clump of clay into a valuable vessel, God can remake our lives if we will put ourselves unreservedly into His hands. He can comfort and soothe us and bind up our wounds. He can restore and renew us. We only have to put the pieces into His hands and let Him do the work. It may be painful, and may take longer than we would like. But the good news for the rejected is that God can give beauty and significance to even the most broken life.

Something beautiful, something good;
All my confusion, He understood;
All I had to offer Him was brokenness and strife,
But He made something beautiful of my life
("Something Beautiful," William J. Gaither and Gloria Gaither, *Hymns for the Family of God,* Paragon, p. 656).

It was the Man of La Mancha who sang the song, "To Dream the Impossible Dream." The heart of that moving play is the interaction between the Man of La Mancha and a common prostitute who captures his fancy. Repeatedly he calls her Dulcinea, "My lady, my love." Yet she snarls back at him in return, retorting with venom, "I am no lady! I am

Aldonza! I am a common whore that men use and throw away! I am nothing!'' Aldonza—a frog in the swamp.

Yet even as she flees from the Man of La Mancha, rejecting his affection, he calls after her, "My lady! Dulcinea! You are my lady!''

As the play closes, Don Quixote lies near death, a broken and destitute man. To his side floats a Spanish princess elegantly dressed in the trappings of royalty. She sits next to him and softly says, "My lord.''

He gazes at her and weakly asks, "Who are you?''

"Why, don't you remember the song you sang, 'To Dream the Impossible Dream'?''

"Yes, I remember the song, but who are you?''

"My lord, I am your lady. I am Dulcinea!''

A rejected, ragtag prostitute had been transformed into a beautiful and elegant princess. By what? By the persistent love of someone who wouldn't quit believing in her, who refused to give up on her. She was transformed by the love of a man who had the courage and the compassion to bend down and kiss a frog. That is exactly what God wants to do for us.

Who wants to kiss a frog? God does—if you will let Him. Put your life in His hands and let Him love you. And do you know what will happen if you do? Crash—Boom—ZAP! Here comes another prince!

7

When Your Blanket Is in the Wash

In January of 1980 the San Jose *Mercury News* published the results of their survey to discover which comic strip was the most popular among the one and a half million people in the Santa Clara Valley. The overwhelming favorite was *Peanuts*. We can't always count on *Tank McNamara* or *Blondie* to give us a laugh. We don't know if *Rex Morgan* or *Mary Worth* will solve our problems. And we can't always be sure we'll understand *Doonesbury*. But we can always count on getting at least a smile out of *Peanuts*.

Those of us who are fans of the Peanuts gang have all chosen a character with whom we most identify. For some of us, it's Charlie Brown, that kind, persevering, sincere, innocent figure who always seems to lose but whom we can't help but love anyway. Some of us identify with Lucy, who has the front of a cold, hard crab, but underneath would like nothing more than to be kissed and loved by Schroeder, the hard-to-get pianist and Beethoven lover. Some of us identify with Snoopy, who seems to enjoy life more than anyone else, and who is able to get away with more because he's so cute. Some may be more comfortable with Pig Pen, who has yet to learn that cleanliness is next to godliness, or with Peppermint Patty, the fatherless tomboy whose baseball team always manages to slaughter the ragamuffin team fielded by Charlie Brown and the gang.

My favorite is Linus. He is never ruffled, and always has an answer for Charlie Brown when Charlie is puzzled about life. He always has an answer for his sister Lucy when she threatens to punch his eyes out. Linus is the personification of Cool. But Linus has a flaw in his character—he is cool only as long as he has his blanket. Take away his blanket and Linus becomes a bundle of nerves.

Linus undergoes a major trauma every two weeks, on the day his blanket, his security, goes into the wash. During that hour, Linus is vulnerable to every unsettling fear that invades his world. His only solution is to stand guard by the washer and dryer, and wait until his source of strength and comfort has finished the last cycle and is returned to him. Like one who has narrowly escaped capture, Linus frantically snatches his blanket from its temporary prison and collapses in a heap of exhaustion.

But the biggest test of Linus' courage comes when Miss Othmar, his school teacher, demands that he not bring his blanket to school. Linus retaliates by proposing a deal: He'll give up his blanket if she will give up biting her nails. Miss Othmar agrees, and the duel is on.

A few days later Linus and Charlie Brown are walking down the street. Linus exclaims, "I didn't think she could *do* it! I didn't think she'd be able to give up chewing her fingernails for five minutes, and here it's been five days!"

Charlie Brown replies, "You judged her wrong, didn't you?"

"I'll say I did," returns Linus. "I made my big mistake when I judged her as a human being instead of as a school teacher."

Did you ever have a security blanket when you were younger? Was it your dog or cat or hamster? Perhaps it *was* a blanket. Or maybe, like me, you had a teddy bear. Boopsy saw me through toilet training, spankings, being laughed at by my playmates, and many a frightening night. But once in a while Boopsy needed to go in for repairs—to have a leg sewn together or an eye replaced. And while Boopsy was in the shop, I was forced to face the terrors and tensions of the world all by myself.

This desire to be secure is a desire to feel safe in the always hectic and sometimes dangerous struggle of life. It is an urge for serenity, for a feeling of calm. It is a desire to know that while the hurricane is swirling all around us, we are safe and protected in the eye of the storm. It's the frantic kicking of the one-year-old climbing off the couch as his feet stretch to find solid ground. It's the need of the five-year-old to be held by mother after falling off his tricycle. It's the hope of us all, that in the middle of our mixed-up lives there is something or someone who can provide stability and balance, who can make sense out of all the nonsense we see. And when Mom isn't there to hold us, when we can't find anything that seems to make sense, when the ground feels as secure as jello in an earthquake, frustration sets in.

You no longer have blankets or teddy bears for security. You've exchanged those vestiges of childhood for more adult things. But how do you deal with the frustration of insecurity when the object of your security is taken away from you? What do you do when your blanket is in the wash?

Security Blankets for Adult Use

One of the most common objects we turn to for our security is *money*. We are convinced that if only we had a stable and abundant supply of money, we could feel safe and at peace. Perhaps the reason we think this way is because most of us have known what it's like to live on the edge financially. We've known the frightening feeling of being in debt. We've felt the pinch. Even now, while we may not be wondering where our next meal is coming from, we may not know how we're going to afford a down payment on a house or be able to send the kids to college. As long as we don't have in hand the funds to *guarantee* that all bills will be paid, we find ourselves feeling insecure.

It would be very comforting to have an unlimited supply of wealth, or a benefactor to bail us out of any tight squeeze, send us on a cruise around the world, and fill our freezers with popsicles.

You may already have a fair degree of financial security. Yet what happens when your husband dies, or when you get laid off, or your business folds? Where is your security, if your money is taken away from you? Money can provide a sense of security, but it can't provide us with the guarantee we all would like.

A second object of our search for security is *relationships*. There is nothing like having people who love you to make you feel secure. God has made us as social creatures. We need other people to let us know that we're OK, to help us develop a sense of identity and esteem. There is no person who feels more insecure than the one who has nobody to love him, to laugh with him, and to listen to his troubles. Though Ann Kiemel has learned how to be secure when her blanket is in the wash, she describes how she sometimes felt, before her marriage, on returning from a speaking engagement:

When I unlock the door to my little apartment,
there is no one to greet me. . .
no strong man to wrap me in his arms,
to laugh with me in love and belonging,
shedding my sophistication.
no one to hear whether I felt encouraged or disappointed
about people's receptiveness to me and my dreams,
no child to scoop up and squeeze
and call my own (*I Love the Word Impossible*,
Tyndale, pp. 15-16).

Just knowing that you have a family who cares about you, even if that family is thousands of miles away, enables you to weather life's storms a bit more confidently. Just knowing there will be someone at the door to wrap his arms around you and cuddle you when you come home from a long day, gives you the strength you need to slog your way through life's mudholes.

Because people are so important to us, we search desperately for someone to love us and care for us, and when we do find them we cling to them tenaciously, like Linus clutching his blanket, so as never to lose them. There's no doubt about it—relationships are a vital source of our security.

But unfortunately, our relationships aren't always able to give us the security we desire. In the introduction of Gail Sheehy's bestseller *Passages*, she describes the event which led her to write her book on the predictable crises of adult life. She was on assignment as a reporter in Northern Ireland at a time when a great deal of fighting was taking place. While she was interviewing a teenage boy on a balcony, just after a peaceful civil rights demonstration, she heard the roar of a gun and watched in horror as the boy's face was ripped off by the bullet. She scrambled to the ground in time to escape the next round of gunfire, but watched helplessly as 13 others were mowed down. In her grief and shock she turned to her source of security, her relationship with her man. She called him long distance in New York to hear his loving voice and words of comfort that would, as she described it, "make all the dangers go away."

But her man didn't have the magic words. His voice sounded cool, breezy, and unconcerned. She was shattered:

From the moment I hung up on that nonconversation, my head went numb. My scalp shrank. Some dark switch was thrown, and a series of weights began to roll across my brain like steel balls. I had squandered my one wish to be saved. . . . "

As I joined the people lying on their stomachs, a powerful idea took hold: No one is with me. No one can keep me safe. There is no one who won't ever leave me alone (E.P. Dutton, pp. 4-5).

What do you do when the relationship you depended on for

security isn't there anymore? A New York psychiatrist Simon Grolnic, compares the relationships we depend on for our security to teddy bears and concludes, "These later-life teddy bears become extremely important, to the point that a person feels worthless without them" (quoted by Christopher Drake in "Why Some Hug Teddy Throughout Their Lives," San Jose *Mercury News*, June 8, 1980). When you move away from friends and family, when your spouse is unfaithful, when a father or a mother dies, your security is stripped away and you are left to fend for yourself. What do you do when your blanket is in the wash?

The third place that many people turn to for security is *achievement*. There are some of us who can get along without having a great deal of money. There are others of us who can get along without having a great number of friends and family to surround and support. But take away our achievements, and our whole foundation collapses. Our sense of worth, our sense of value, our sense of security is totally dependent on what we have accomplished.

Gail Sheehy marvelously captures the essence of this kind of a person in her description of what she calls the "wunderkind."

Money is often a secondary motive in the whirlwind life of the wunderkind. The main thrust is to enter the inner circle. They make this happen by subordinating everything else to the drive to be Number One, whereupon, they expect, their insecurities will vanish, they will be loved and admired, and nobody can humiliate them or denigrate them or make them feel dependent ever again (*Passages,* pp. 275-276).

Children are motivated to achieve by a desire to gain the love and attention of parents. Adolescents are motivated by the desire to gain the love and admiration of peers, particularly peers of the opposite sex. But adults are not motivated by any person in particular. It's the whole world they are trying to impress, "the generalized others." Adults want people they have never met to know of and admire them, and the best way to gain the admiration of "the generalized others" is through achievement.

The trap the high achiever falls into is that of never being satisfied with what he's accomplished. Soren Kierkegaard once remarked, "When a man aspires to be a Caesar and fails to become a Caesar, he will hate what he is because he is not Caesar" (quoted by Anthony Campolo, Jr. in *The Success Fantasy,* Victor, p. 74). The achiever isn't satisfied with doing well. He must be the best, the greatest, the biggest.

But what happens when the achiever fails? What happens when the executive fails to become vice-president, when the athlete misses the game-winning free throw, when the musician fails to get his songs recorded? What happens when by your measure of success you fall short?

The Cure for Insecurity—Wisdom

God's cure for our ailment is found in the Book of Proverbs. The focus of Proverbs 3 is on wisdom and understanding.

My son, let them not depart from your sight;
  Keep sound wisdom and discretion;
So they will be life to your soul,
  and adornment to your neck.
Then you will walk your way securely,
  and your foot will not stumble.
When you lie down, you will not be afraid;
  when you lie down, your sleep will be sweet.
Do not be afraid of sudden fear,
  nor of the onslaught of the wicked, when it comes;
for the Lord will be your confidence,
  and will keep your foot from being caught
                              (Prov. 3:21-26).

The cure for insecurity is *wisdom.* Solomon tells us that if we cling to wisdom, if we hold wisdom tightly to us like a charm hanging around our necks, then we will walk on our way securely. Then we won't stumble. Then we can sleep unafraid.

The wise person doesn't lie awake at night worrying about what might happen if he fails a test or if he doesn't finish the project for work on schedule. The wise person doesn't fret and fume about whether or not he is better than somebody else, about whether or not he is loved and admired by the right people. The wise person doesn't come unglued when his finances get tight or his best friend moves or his business venture fails. The wise person is secure.

But what is wisdom? What does it mean to be wise? Wisdom is not merely the accumulation of knowledge but the ability to use knowledge in the practical situations of life. Wisdom is the wedding of knowing and doing. The wise person not only knows what is right—he does it. He lives out what he knows. He lives the truth he has discovered. Wisdom is truth for living.

Yet it is important to clarify the nature of that truth. It is not the truth about Watergate as seen by Howard Hunt or Gordon Liddy. It is not the truth about Three Mile Island as told by the Nuclear Regulatory Commission. It is not the truth about life after death as told by someone who has been "beyond and back." It is God's truth. It is reality as viewed from God's perspective. Wisdom is learning to view life from the perspective of the One who created us and knows all about us. The wise person, who has acquired truth by viewing life from God's perspective, is able to put that truth into action as he sets his priorities and lives his life. When we see life from the perspective of our Creator, then we will be secure.

Because the wise person sees life from God's perspective, he knows that there is a firm foundation under his feet. Even though the ground might shake a bit, even though he might have his legs knocked out from under him from time to time, even though things might not always make perfect sense to him, he still knows that the God who rules the universe is a Rock who will never crumble. He knows that he has a shelter, a refuge, a protection that can't be penetrated.

The psalmist wrote of the person who had placed his life in God's hands:

Whoever goes to the Lord for safety,
Whoever remains under the protection of the Almighty, can say to Him, "You are my defender and protector. You are my God; in You I trust." He will keep you safe from all hidden dangers and from all deadly diseases. He will cover you with His wings; you will be safe in His care; His faithfulness will protect and defend you. You need not fear any dangers of night or sudden attacks during the day or the plagues that strike in the dark or the evils that kill in daylight.
A thousand may fall dead beside you, ten thousand all around you, but you will not be harmed" (Ps. 91:1-7, GNB).

While everything around him is caving in, the person who has put his life into God's hands and who bases his life on God's values, is secure in the knowledge that God is his protector.

How To View Life From God's Perspective

What does it mean to view life from God's perspective? How do we do it? What is God's perspective?

In order to be as practical as possible, let's look at God's perspective on those objects we so often turn to for our security. What value or priority does He place on them? And how does He want us to relate to them?

● First, what is God's point of view about *money*? If you begin reading through the Bible looking for God's attitudes about money and possessions, you will discover that He has a great deal to say about it. God cares about things like property ownership, interest, investments, welfare, taxes, and benevolent contributions. The Bible teaches that the way we manage our property is a distinct indicator of spiritual maturity. It is important that we properly value and efficiently use our financial resources. Yet we are reminded not to become too attached to our possessions: "Beware, and be on your guard against every form of greed; for not even when one has an abundance does his life consist of his possessions" (Luke 12:15).

Perhaps the most comprehensive statement in the Bible on this subject is from the Apostle Paul:

Instruct those who are rich in this present world not to be conceited or to fix their hope on the uncertainty of riches, but on God, who richly supplies us with all things to enjoy. Instruct them to do good, to be rich in good works, to be generous and ready to share, storing up for themselves the treasure of a good foundation for the future, so that they may take hold of that which is life indeed" (1 Tim. 6:17-19).

Yet there is a principle that I feel is important to share with you. A number of very successful people have told me that if I follow this principle I will most certainly be a wealthy person, no matter what I pursue. Their principle of success is this: meet people's needs.

Meet people's needs. Scratch people where they itch. How simple, but how true! The product that best meets perceived need sells the best. The cleanser that gets spots and stains out of carpeting better than any other cleanser will be the most successful one. The salesman who gives the best service will be successful.

God's word of wisdom to us is this: meet people's needs, be a servant, and you will be on your way to financial provision. God doesn't promise us instant wealth, but He does promise that all of our financial needs will be met more than adequately: "You will be made rich in every way so that you can be generous on every occasion, and through us your generosity will result in thanksgiving to God" (2 Cor. 9:11, NIV). The wise person meets the needs of people.

● What is God's perspective on *relationships?* God created us as social beings. We need to love and be loved, to know and be known. We thrive on intimacy. We yearn for people we can trust, who care enough to listen to us, who are interested in what happens to us today.

In a chapter prologue in his book *The Secret of Staying in Love,* John Powell quotes Viktor Frankl, the eminent psychologist:

A thought transfixed me: For the first time in my life I saw the truth as it is set into song by so many poets, proclaimed as the final wisdom by so many thinkers. The truth—that love is the ultimate and highest goal to which man can aspire. Then I grasped the meaning of the greatest secret that human poetry and human thought and belief have to impart: the salvation of man is through love and in love (Argus, p. 42).

God has designed us so that we might be able to experience the ecstasy of being loved and the joy of loving. The wise person is willing to love and be loved.

But he is also aware that no individual can meet all his needs or satisfy all his desires. There is no husband in the world who can meet all the needs of his wife. There is no friend in the world who can live up to all of your expectations. There isn't anyone who will always be sensitive to *my* feelings, who will always keep all his promises, who will always be there to listen to me. The wise person is willing to love and trust his family and friends without demanding that they perfectly fulfill all of his desires.

The wise person also knows the secret of friendship. He knows that if he meets people's needs, he will have more trustworthy, loving, dependable friends than he will be able to handle.

Who are the people you get along with the best and care for the most? They are probably the people who know you well and care about you enough to be able to meet your needs, to encourage you, advise you, comfort you, and make you laugh. They are the people who will spend their day off helping you move or build a patio. They offer to baby-sit for your three youngsters so that you can go out for dinner. They are willing to watch slides from your vacation. People who care about people, who are servants, who meet other people's needs, will experience the joys of intimacy and of love.

While I was in college my roommate's girlfriend came to me one day with what I thought was a unique problem. She explained that in the previous week 11 people had told her they considered her their best friend. Nancy just didn't have time for so many best friends. She was finding it difficult to study because her friends were always knocking on her door or calling her on the phone.

As she told me her situation I thought, Why is little Nancy Jane so popular? She is cute, but not beautiful. She isn't doing well in school and doesn't know what she wants to do, if and when she graduates. She's completely tone deaf and an embarrassment to us all when she sings. Why do people flock to her?

Nancy Jane was popular because people knew she cared. When Nancy asked you how you were, she really wanted to know and was willing to take the time to listen. If there was ever something she could do to cheer you up or help you out, she would drop everything and give you her undivided attention. Because she was interested in meeting people's needs, she had a problem more of us would like—she had too many friends! Meet people's needs, serve people, and your life will be full of good and satisfying friendships.

● What is God's perspective on *achievement?* There is no doubt that God desires for His people to be successful. There is no doubt that He wants us to do our best, to not settle for the mediocre but "go for the gold." There is no doubt that we are to dream big dreams, dedicate ourselves to pursuing our dreams, and then do everything in our power to make them come true.

Yet the wise person knows that there will be times when his gifts aren't enough to make his dreams come true. He recognizes that there are limitations to his abilities and resources, and that because of those limitations or certain unforeseen circumstances, he will fail to reach his goals. The wise person is willing to dream and attempt great things, aware that he is risking failure, because he knows that his security and worth do not depend on success.

The wise man also knows that there is a secret to success—that if he meets people's needs he will be a success in whatever he does, no matter how high the risk of failure.

Jesus articulated this secret to His disciples, for they were concerned with becoming great. Jesus made it clear to them that they could be successful, could become great, but that there was a cost to be paid: "Whoever wishes to become great among you shall be your servant, and whoever wishes to be first among you shall be your slave; just as the Son of man did not come to be served, but to serve, and to give His life a ransom for many" (Matt. 20:26-28). The secret to success is in serving, in meeting people's needs.

In *The Success Fantasy*, Dr. Tony Campolo notes that for most people, success means acquiring wealth, power, and prestige. He points out that such a definition of success is quite contrary to God's perspective on the matter:

On Judgment Day, the Lord will reveal the value of actions that seemed relatively unimportant. He will give special recognition to those who fed the hungry, clothed the naked, visited the sick and the imprisoned, and will declare that those who have done such things are the most blessed in the kingdom of God. . . . Many men have found success in taking advantage of opportunities to express love in simple ways. It is more important to express love in little things that we do for one another day by day than to gain fame in the eyes of the world" (Victor, pp. 88-89).

How can we be secure when our blanket is in the wash? By clinging to wisdom. And wisdom is viewing life from God's perspective. How do we get wisdom? By getting to know the source of wisdom—God:

For the Lord gives wisdom;
　from His mouth come knowledge and understanding.
He stores up sound wisdom for the upright;
　He is a shield to those who walk in integrity,
guarding the paths of justice,
　and He preserves the way of His godly ones (Prov.
2:6-8).

The only enduring source of security is a relationship with God. When we put God first in our lives and make His values our values, we will be secure. But when the elements of our lives are out of proper perspective—when money or possessions, achievements or even people become our overriding and primary passions, taking precedence over everything else, including God—we can be sure that insecurity is only a breath behind.

Is your blanket in the wash? Don't worry—you don't need it anymore! Let God take its place, and have a good night's sleep. God is your security. He is the only Rock that will never ever crumble.

8

Just Another Brick in the Wall

"All in all, you're just another brick in the wall," sang the rock group Pink Floyd, in the early 1980s. And with those words, they captured the gnawing feeling that haunts adolescents and adults alike.

The evidence certainly suggests that each of us is indeed just another brick in the wall. The 1980 census revealed that I am one in a city of 620,000 people, in a state of 23 million, in a world of 4.5 billion, a number which will double in 20 years.

Astronomers tell us that our sun is just one of 100 billion stars in the Milky Way galaxy, and that our galaxy is only one of a billion galaxies in our universe. This is interpreted to mean that the chances of Earth being the only inhabited planet in the universe are very, very slim.

In the Western World, we have discovered not only that we are each one of a large number, but also that we each *are* a number.

Lest I bore you, just a few of my numbers are: 1-809-5672-5; 34-474-789; 677-922; and AW 76232734. And you have your own list of numbers by which the government and creditors know you.

Maybe we are not even bricks in the wall—just numbers

from a math book! This frustrates our desire to feel significant and worthwhile. We resent being treated as a number or thing. Deep inside each of us, a small voice is aching to inform anyone who will listen that we are special and unique and worthy of their attention. Yet before we can convince the world of our significance, we need to be convinced of it ourselves.

How hard it is to believe our worth, when we are embarrassed even to stand in front of the bathroom mirror. How hard it is to believe that we count, when our skills and abilities and qualifications add up to so little in comparison with the person at the next desk. How hard it is to believe that we are good and valuable people, when our failures and foibles are replayed nightly on the screen that is drawn when we close our eyes to sleep.

The desire to feel good about who we are and who we are becoming, to feel that our lives have substance and beauty, is so often frustrated by the most pervading psychological problem of our time, low self-esteem. Instead of feeling good about ourselves, we feel bad. Instead of feeling valuable, we feel worthless. Instead of feeling significant, we feel like just another brick in the wall.

Recovery from a negative self-image is long and arduous, but by the power of God it is possible. If you will carefully work your way through this chapter and follow the principles offered, you can see your frustration turned into the fulfillment of a healthy, positive, growing self-esteem. It will take work, the grace of God, and some help from people who care, but in time it *can* happen.

It's OK to Want to Feel OK

The first truth that we must become convinced of is that it's OK to want to feel OK. It isn't sin, or a mark of arrogance or selfishness to want to feel that my life is significant and that I am a very important and special person. In fact, just the opposite is true! If I think that I am insignificant and unimportant, I sin, because I am calling God a liar. God has said I am important enough to send His Son to die for me. Jesus reminded His disciples, "Are not five sparrows sold for two cents? And yet not one of them is forgotten before God. Indeed, the very hairs of your head are all numbered. Do not fear; you are of more value than many sparrows" (Luke 12:6-7).

The psalmist was convinced of human value: "When I consider Thy heavens, the work of Thy fingers, the moon and the stars, which Thou hast ordained; what is man that Thou dost take thought of him? And the son of man, that Thou dost care for him? Yet Thou hast made him little lower than God, and dost crown him with glory and majesty! Thou dost make him to rule over the works of Thy hands; Thou hast put all things under his feet" (Ps. 8:3-6).

How important are we? Important enough to be crowned with glory and honor, to have all the rest of God's creation placed under our rule. How special are we? So special that we are just a "little lower than God!" Is it OK to want to feel significant and special? Why not? We are special!

It is much more than just OK to want to feel good about who we are—it is essential! Dr. William Glasser, author of *Reality Therapy*, has proposed two fundamental assumptions about our sense of personal worth. His first assumption is that *all* psychological problems, from the slightest neuroses to the deepest psychoses, are symptomatic of the frustration of our fundamental need for a sense of personal worth. His second assumption is that the self-image of any individual will be the basic determining factor of all his behavior. Lloyd John Ogilvie explains this second assumption when he says, "How we think results in how we feel; and how we feel dictates what we do. Until we know we are loved and are free to love, we will cause disruption and distortion all around us" (*Loved and Forgiven*, Regal, p. 37). In other words, how I act, how I treat other people, is a result of how I think and feel about myself.

How does a person with a low self-image, who thinks of himself as insignificant and unworthy, act and relate? In a variety of ways. He may exaggerate and brag about himself in an attempt to build up his own image. He may become extremely critical of others, hoping to elevate himself by lowering others. He may become a perfectionist; he may be extremely shy and introverted; he may be self-depreciating; he may become depressed, or he may be angry.

Dr. Anthony Campolo has asserted, "As a sociologist, I am convinced that feeling like a failure at school is a major cause of juvenile delinquency" (*The Success Fantasy*, Victor, p. 38). The student who feels unsuccessful as a person may choose to ventilate the pain he feels through antisocial behavior. Philosopher Bertrand Russell stated the point succinctly when he said, "A man cannot possibly be at peace with others until he has learned to be at peace with himself" (quoted by John Powell in *The Secret of Staying in Love*, Argus, p. 16).

The person with a negative self-image may choose yet another option—physical illness. The pain of failure or of feeling worthless is transferred into physical symptoms, for these are easier for a person to handle with a vestige of dignity than are emotional outbursts. Some have even suggested that as much as 90 percent of all physical illness is psychologically induced! Is it OK to want to feel OK? For our mental health, our physical well-being, and our spiritual wholeness, it is *essential*. God's desire for each of us is that we feel that our lives are significant and special. While we may not always seem loveable, God wants us to know that we are certainly worth loving.

Why Don't I Feel OK?

Once we have discovered that it's all right to want to feel OK, it is helpful to understand some of the reasons why we don't feel OK. What makes me feel like just another brick in the wall? Why do I hate what I am? Why am I so shy? Why am I so critical of others? Why do I feel so worthless?

There are at least nine possible sources of a negative self-image, nine possible reasons why we feel insignificant, unimportant, and unloved.

• The first source is the failure of parents and other significant people from our early years to adequately convey love and acceptance to us. This is not to assign all of the blame for a poor self-image to parents, but merely to recognize the importance that they play in the development of a child's self-respect.

For children, a primary motivation is gaining the approval and affection of their parents. Children will do anything to make their parents proud of them. Yet many parents, in a sincere attempt to motivate their children, have chosen the technique of withholding affirmation. Instead of applauding their child's efforts, they withhold their approval in order to motivate their child to do even better. Meanwhile the distraught child feels like nothing he ever has done or could do would be good enough to please his parents.

Without meaning to, many parents retard the development of a positive self-image in their children. My own father often let me know he loved me and was proud of me, and that I was very special to him. But he was also an extreme perfectionist. While he was obviously pleased when I did well on my report card, his first question was always, "Why didn't you get an A in this class?" Dad was very talented in building and repairing things, and on a number of occasions tried to teach me the skills he had learned. But because of his compulsion to see things done perfectly, I never finished any of the projects I began. Dad would always step in and redo what I had done or add some finishing touches to something I thought was just fine. I eventually concluded that I couldn't please him, that I couldn't do anything well enough to earn his complete approval. I became so afraid of doing something wrong that I simply quit trying to learn the skills that Dad had set out to teach me.

I have never blamed him for the insecurity I developed

about myself. But in looking back, I realize that one of the reasons I have always had a morbid fear of failure and a passionate compulsion to achieve is because of my relationship with my father. As I grew up, the message was indirectly communicated to me that anything less than perfection was failure and failure would not be tolerated. To be fully accepted and loved, I needed to succeed in school, in athletics, and in life as a whole. But I was also a very fortunate child. For while I could never completely please my father, I knew that he loved me and in the long run, was on my side.

Many children never do receive the love and affirmation they want and work for so diligently. Psychologists suggest that unless children receive parental approval in the preadolescent period, they find it very difficult to allow anyone else to take the place of their parents as significant others. Some people live their whole lives in a futile attempt to gain the approval of their parents. One of the reasons some young girls become prostitutes is to punish their fathers for never having given them the affection and approval they so desperately need. The unconditional love of parents is essential to the development of a child's healthy and positive self-image.

• The second possible source of a low self-esteem is the lack of affirmation and encouragement youngsters often experience in school. After talking with scores of people about their early school years, I believe that everyone has felt the excruciating pain of failing in school. In those early years children are especially eager to please their teachers, as well as to be accepted and admired by peers. A few doses of failure and ridicule during those years are enough to leave scars that remain for a long time.

Through the story of Arnie and the spelling contest, Dr. James Dobson very sensitively enables those who read his book *Hide or Seek* or see his *Focus on the Family* films to appreciate the effect of a traumatic school experience. Arnie is the local dummy and no one wants him on their spelling team. Finally the teacher assigns Arnie to a team and, sure enough,

Arnie flubs the first word and is exiled to his desk and to boos from his team.

But it isn't just Arnie who has his self-image damaged. It's Mary and John as well, the smart kids who are the captains. Sooner or later, Mary and John will fail at something, and they will feel the same pain that Arnie felt. They won't feel it as often, but it will hurt just as much.

When I was in grade school I was the captain of our spelling team. While I'm sure we won our share of spelling bees, the only one I really remember is the one we lost—or more accurately, I lost. Our class was having a spelling bee against another class down the hall. My teacher and my classmates were all counting on me, their champion speller, to lead them to a glorious victory. But early in the game, I choked. The teacher asked me to spell prophet, like the ones in the Bible. But the only word that I could picture was spelled p-r-o-f-i-t. The teacher was so sure that I could get it right that even after I spelled it wrong the first time, she gave me another chance. I felt everyone looking at me. I carried their hopes for victory in this all-important spelling bee. But the right letters wouldn't come. To the groans of my team, the loud cheers of the other team, and the obvious disappointment of my teacher who had such high expectations for me, I ran to my desk and buried my head in my arms, tears streaking down my face. It was a wound that hurt deeply and which took a long time to heal.

At some time or another each of us has had an experience similar to Arnie's and to mine, one which has significantly influenced how we think and feel about ourselves. Somewhere along the line we've all been scolded by a teacher, glared at for causing a disruption, or upbraided for failing to do an assignment. And each time that happened, the good feeling that we had about ourselves died just a little bit.

● A third source of our negative self-image is the exaggerated and warped stress placed by our society on values that are not scriptural. As Dobson points out, in our society appearance is the primary means of evaluating an individual's worth. The physically beautiful person is deemed more valuable than the ugly person. The beautiful person receives more affirmation—and more frequent raises. The plain or ugly person is left to fend for himself.

Other factors that our society uses to evaluate worth are intelligence, skill, wealth, heritage, and status. The Stanford graduate is a more important person than the graduate of a small college in Iowa. The vice-president of the company is worth more than her secretary. If we happen to be plain-looking, of average intelligence, and have no outstanding skills, heritage, or position to distinguish ourselves, we quite naturally conclude that we aren't as significant or important as an attractive, intelligent executive.

● The fourth source of a negative self-image is pride. Pride is a product of comparing ourselves with others. Pride isn't satisfied with being as good as someone else; it demands that we be better than the next person.

Pastor Erwin Lutzer tells us that "pride produces insecurity. It magnifies the desire for recognition and influence and enlarges personal ambition beyond reason. . . . The legitimate need for acceptance has been turned into the bondage of selfish desire" (*How in This World Can I be Holy?* Moody, p. 25).

In *True Spirituality*, Francis Schaeffer suggests that the person victimized by pride lives on a pendulum. When the pendulum swings one way, he feels superior to others. When it swings back again, he feels inferior. It is because of his need to feel superior to everyone that he always ends up feeling inferior. No matter how we might excel in something, there is always someone better. There is always someone more beautiful, more skillful, more persuasive, more muscular, and when we meet that person our feeling of inferiority is magnified a thousand times because we wanted so badly to be the best.

● The fifth source of a negative self-image is true guilt. While the cross of Jesus Christ stands as a beacon to proclaim that we are worth dying for, it also stands as a warning. Jesus died because we are sinners. We are guilty. We have broken God's commandments and we have offended our friends and neighbors. When we look at ourselves honestly, we see a guilty, sinful person. Sometimes we feel bad about ourselves simply because we have done something bad. It doesn't take us long to reason that anyone who does bad things is a bad person, and the jump to "I am insignificant" and "I am worthless" is but a small step.

• A sixth source of a negative self-image is the influence of the society we live in and its emphasis on largeness. We shop in monolithic shopping centers, work for gigantic corporations, attend mammoth universities, and belong to enormous churches. Wherever we go, we are lost in the thousands of other consumers, employees, students, and parishioners.

• The seventh source of a negative self-image is our society's emphasis on competition. Because we have learned that acceptance is competitively earned, it is difficult for us to accept love that is unconditional. We want to be deserving of God's love, we want to earn the respect and acceptance of our peers. Many of us do not feel loved until we have achieved something that makes us feel that we are worth that love.

• Failure and rejection are both sources and results of negative self-image. The person who fails at some venture that is important to him, whether it be a spelling contest or a presidential election, can't help but have his ego wounded. The hurt can heal, but in the meantime the pain can be torturous, and the scars may remain. A person can recover from being rejected, but if he is rejected often enough, he can't help but conclude that there is something seriously wrong with him.

The Key to Self-Esteem: Acceptance

Our recognition of the sources of our feelings of unworthiness and insignificance is a notable step in developing a more healthy and positive self-image. If we have an accurate idea of why we feel bad about ourselves, then we are able to take more effective steps toward resolving a negative self-image. A familiar adage states, "A problem well-defined is a problem half solved." If your feelings of inferiority or worthlessness have their roots in certain childhood experiences, then just the fact that you are able to identify those experiences will enable you to begin the process of healing.

Yet while it is helpful to recognize the roots of our negative self-image, much more than that is needed to make the jump from the frustration of feeling worthless to the fulfillment of experiencing the positive and healthy self-esteem that God intended us to have.

The Gospel tells us that God is able and willing to get down on His hands and knees to help us wherever we hurt. He is anxious for us to experience His love and power and grace. But because He is loving and gracious Himself, He does not force Himself on us. He always waits until we respond to His offer to help. The key to unlock the healing power of God in our lives is acceptance. Before we will be able to accept ourselves, we must first accept God's forgiveness, God's values, God's truth, and God's love.

● First, we must accept God's *forgiveness*. Since one of the sources of our unhealthy self-image is true guilt, it is imperative that we have a deep experience of God's forgiveness. In discussing this issue Dr. Robert Schuller has said that what "keeps people from loving themselves is the problem of guilt. There is no self-esteem until I have had an experience of being declared to be righteous and then suddenly in the mind of God—I am treated as perfect" ("Self-Love: How Far? How Biblical? How Healthy?" *Eternity*, February 1979, p. 22).

The Bible teaches that when we sincerely confess our sin and failure to God, He forgives us. He wipes the slate clean so that in His eyes we are perfect. He sees us as if we had never sinned in the first place, as if we had been perfect all along! God's forgiveness is total and without reservation.

Yet it is up to us to accept that forgiveness. To continue to try to earn what is already ours is futile. And yet so often

Christians try to earn God's forgiveness and grace by being more active, giving more, or studying the Bible more.

Joseph Cooke was a missionary to Thailand for many years. After years of preaching, teaching, studying, and giving, Joseph Cooke finally could give no more. He had a nervous breakdown and was so shattered by the experience that he could hardly bring himself to pray or read the Bible.

How could such a thing happen to a dedicated missionary? It happened to Joseph Cooke because, as he describes it, "life was one long, deadly grind of trying to be perfect to earn the daily pleasure of a God who simply could not be pleased. His demands were so high and His opinion of me so low that there was no way I could really live under anything but His frown" ("The God of Nervous Breakdowns," *The Christian Reader*, May/June 1979, p. 76).

The Gospel tells us that God smiles on us. Once we repent of our sins and commit our lives to Him, He washes away all of our sin—past, present, and future. There is nothing we can do to earn God's forgiveness or favor. He's already given it to us. All we have to do is accept it.

• In order to accept ourselves we must learn to accept God's *values*. We must affirm that the internal beauty of a godly character is more to be valued than the external beauty of an attractive body. We must affirm that each one of us is of infinite value, no matter what our background, educational level, talents, or resources. God does not discriminate against us for any reason, and we should not devalue ourselves.

Accepting God's values also includes accepting our *limitations*. Many of God's people are handicapped in one way or another. Many have been crippled through disease or accident. Many of us are not extraordinarily intelligent or attractive or talented. God made most of us to be quite ordinary, and some even weak and quite unattractive. Most of us will never compose a great symphony, perform on nationwide television, become respected senators, or invent amazing new products. We can accept our limitations because we know God has designed each of us just as we are for a very special purpose. Paul explained this in writing to the Corinthian church:

For consider your calling, brethren; not many of you were wise according to worldly standards, not many were powerful, not many were of noble birth; but God chose what is foolish in the world to shame the wise, God chose what is weak in the world to shame the strong, God chose what is low and despised in the world, even things that are not, to bring to nothing things that are, so that no human being might boast in the presence of God" (1 Cor. 1:26-29, RSV).

Paul delivered his conclusion to the matter in his second letter: "But we have this treasure in earthen vessels, to show that the transcendent power belongs to God and not to us" (2 Cor. 4:7, RSV). Why did God give one person a puny, unattractive body? And another person a handicap? Why didn't God give you more intelligence, resources, or contacts with influential people? To demonstrate that the transcendent power belongs only to God. Our limitations don't make us any less significant. They do give God a showcase for His power and glory.

The person who has accepted God's values doesn't need to compete or compare himself with others. He doesn't need to come unglued when he meets someone whose talents surpass his own. He needn't be a slave to pride which tells him that he *must* be better than everyone else. The person who has accepted God's values is able to accept himself as he is and others as they are. And finally, the person who has accepted God's values realizes that he is still in progress. He knows that God is molding him into a better person, and that the process of molding takes time.

● We must accept the *truth* about ourselves as it has been spoken by God. The truth is that we are valuable, significant, and unique. The truth is that God created each of us just as we are, that He was involved intimately in every detail of putting us together. Not only did He create us; He also gifted us. The

Bible teaches that we have been given gifts by the Holy Spirit so that we might serve others and glorify God.

When the great architect Christopher Wren walked through the building site of St. Paul's Cathedral in London, he stopped to ask a number of the workers what they were doing. One explained that he was doing carpentry, another that he was laying bricks, and another that he was carving stone. As he left the cathedral Wren met a man mixing mortar and asked him what he was doing. Not realizing that he was speaking to the famous architect of the building the man proudly explained, "Sir, I am building a great cathedral!" (Campolo, *The Success Fantasy*, p. 81)

In order to accept ourselves and enjoy a healthy self-esteem, we must accept the truth about ourselves as spoken by God, the truth that we all have been created and gifted for a very special and significant purpose. We are not just bricks in the wall. We are workers with God in building a great cathedral. Our gifts may seem to pale to insignificance in comparison with the gifts of others, but without us, God's cathedral will never be built.

● We must accept God's *love*. A pastor in a small western town had a very resentful and rebellious son who rejected every word of advice or act of love from his parents. One night the pastor went into his son's bedroom, which was filled with the fumes of alcohol, and observed his wife kneeling next to their son, stroking his hair and kissing and caressing his forehead. Looking up in tears she explained, "He won't let me love him when he's awake" (W. Ross Foley, *You Can Win Over Weariness*, Regal, p. 161).

Perhaps the reason that we find ourselves struggling with powerful, agonizing feelings of self-hate, of inferiority, of insignificance and depression, is that we have simply never let God love us. We've heard that He loves us. We've read it in the Bible and studied it in books. But we've never really accepted it, never really allowed God to surround us and fill us with His unconditional and healing love. The loudest, most persistent, most profound message of the Bible is that God loves you. Accept that love by committing your life in a fresh way to Jesus Christ and asking Him to fill you with His love.

• But there is one more step for the individual lacking a positive self-esteem. After accepting God's forgiveness, values, truth, and love, that person must take a very risky, fearful, but necessary step. He needs to *give* himself away in love and service, focusing on meeting the needs and healing the hurts of others.

According to Robert Schuller, "There is no self-esteem without sacrifice. . . . There is no self-esteem without a cross" ("Self-Love," p. 22). Jesus Christ taught His disciples this truth right from the beginning: "If any man would come after Me, let him deny himself and take up his cross daily and follow Me. For whoever would save his life will lose it; and whoever loses his life for My sake, he will save it" (Luke 9:23-24, RSV).

Where does self-esteem find its roots? In looking out for number one, pulling your own strings, asserting your own rights? No! Self-esteem is not developed by self-assertion. True self-esteem is found in giving love, in helping others to see their own beauty. True self-esteem comes from losing your life, from committing yourself unreservedly to serving God and man: "There is no self-esteem without sacrifice. . . . There is no self-esteem without a cross."

Just another brick in the wall? Not on your life! You are special! You are needed! You are loved! You are a child of God!

9

When the Pain Persists

The experience of pain is not an option for human beings—it is an inescapable fact of life. Stubbed toes, stomachaches from too much candy, and scraped knees are badges of growing up. Tension headaches, heartburn, and backaches are regarded as proofs of having attained the privileges and pressures of adulthood.

While for most of us pain is fortunately limited to the role of an intermittent, unwelcome intruder, for many it is a very faithful and unappreciated companion. This realization was imposed on me one evening when I plopped down comfortably into my favorite recliner to read the local paper and came across the following paragraph:

As you read this, 65 million Americans are enduring lives made almost unbearable by unremitting, agonizing pain. You may be one, or you may know someone who is. Chronic pain of various kinds is America's hidden epidemic. And only those who have lived with its debilitating effects can know the helplessness and frustration that comes from being told by doctor after doctor: "I'm sorry, there's little we can do" (Lawrence Galton, "Science Scores New Victories Over Pain," *Parade*, August 31, 1980, p. 8).

It doesn't take much living to learn that pain is not limited to the human body; the mind and the spirit are also fair game. While you may never have been victimized by the chronic physical pain endured by so many people in our world, chances are very good that in one way or another you have had the opportunity to learn firsthand the meaning of the word *pain*. In her book *Affliction*, Edith Schaeffer explains that our experience of pain, extends far beyond the sensation of physical suffering. She asserts:

An affliction can be physical, psychological, material, emotional, intellectual, or cultural. An affliction can be having too much or too little, having too many demands upon one or no feeling of being needed. An affliction can be a sudden shock or a daily, constant dragging with no change. An affliction can be planned by some human being who wants to do us harm, or can apparently come with no explanation at all (Revell, p. 111).

One of the people I visit regularly is a 28-year-old woman named Susie. She experiences some discomfort, but fairly little physical pain. And yet pain is a daily experience for Susie and her parents. For over five years Susie has been confined to bed with multiple sclerosis.

She is unable to talk, see, eat, sit up, or walk. Her existence is limited to her room and the few trips she makes during the year to be treated by specialists at Stanford Medical Center. Susie's pain is not the stabbing, gnawing pain of a person whose body suffers from cancer, but it is pain nevertheless.

I also visit a 75-year-old man named Walter. After a series of strokes, Walter recently discovered that he has cancer. His pain *is* physical, a pain that throbs with every halting step that he takes. His wife, though physically healthy, bears the pain that comes from knowing that her partner of 47 years is dying and there's nothing she can do about it.

Another person I counsel with on occasion is a 35-year-old woman, a Ph.D. from Stanford and a successful psychologist. Five years ago her husband divorced her, and in the ensuing custody trial pulled out all the stops to gain custody of their two daughters. She suffers the pain of a mother who is not allowed to watch her children grow up, who is not allowed to dress them or feed them or hold them or give a birthday party for them. Her attempts to reverse the court's decision have all failed, and there is little reason to hope that the situation will ever change. Her pain of being involuntarily separated from her own children goes on.

The desire to live a healthy, whole, satisfying life finds itself frustrated over and over again by pain in one form or another. Whether it is physical pain caused by a disease or an accident, or psychological pain of losing a spouse to death, divorce, or desertion, the effect is very much the same. Pain deprives us of the fullness of life we ache so much to enjoy.

Much of the time our bodies and our emotions are very capable of dealing with pain. When it first strikes our defenses come quickly to the rescue. But when the pain persists and our normal problem-solving skills don't seem to do any good, a crisis occurs. We don't know where to turn or what to think.

Time is the great healer, we hear. But what happens when time lets us down, when the pain goes on and on, relentlessly taunting our helplessness? If only there were something. But there is nothing. The piercing, persistent pain shrivels our spirits and riddles our bodies, and refuses to be healed or even pacified by any conventional balm.

What becomes of the abundant life, of joy and laughter and love and peace, when the pain persists?

To a person victimized by persistent pain, the message of the Gospel resonates loudly throughout God's Word: There is always hope! There is no night so dark that the stars do not still shine, no hole so deep that God is not deeper still. God does not promise to always deliver us from the source of our pain, but He does promise to always provide us with the resources we need to live above our painful circumstances. The frustration of pain need not be final. Fulfillment is possible even in pain.

God's Gift—Emotions

There are three very important steps we can take when we find ourselves overwhelmed by some crisis situation in which we are seemingly unable to cope. The first step is to *ventilate our emotions.*

Much has been written in recent years about the danger of repressing our emotions and the need to ventilate them. Even so, it is a concept that is very much misunderstood.

To ventilate our emotions does not mean that it is necessary to verbalize every feeling or act out every emotion. It does not mean that the moment we realize we are feeling angry we must excuse ourselves from the committee meeting to go beat our fists into the pillow we keep in the office for just such occasions. It does not mean that it is mandatory to cry each time we feel sad.

To ventilate our emotions means, first of all, that we must be willing to admit that they are there. It means to be willing to "own" how we feel, to honestly admit that whether we like it or not, we are feeling angry or depressed or guilty or ecstatic.

It is not unhealthy to control how we display our emotions. It is unhealthy to deny that we have them. The first essential for ventilating our emotions is simply to admit to ourselves that we have them, to say to ourselves, "I'm angry," or "I feel cheated."

The second essential for ventilating our emotions is to express them in a constructive, proper way. While it is a mark of maturity to be able to control the way we display our emotions, it is an act of self-destruction to never allow those emotions to surface. Our emotions must find a means of expression. If we don't take the time to express them wisely and constructively, they will find their own way to be released.

It is no secret that pent-up emotions often choose to express their presence through our bodies. When we bottle up our grief or our fear or our anger for too long, our bodies often pay the price in the form of colitis, persistent headaches, or an ulcer. Our bodies may become victims of diseases brought on by the weakened physical state our volatile emotions can produce.

Besides doing damage to our bodies, bottled-up emotions have the capacity to do damage to our relationships. At least once a month something is said or done in our church that causes a strong emotional reaction in me. Being a person who prides himself on his self-control, I rarely respond directly to the person or event that triggered that emotion. Usually I bottle it up and take it home with me.

But without fail that emotion demands to be expressed in some way. If I neglect to vent it in a constructive, appropriate manner, it may come out in an irrational eruption at my wife because her chocolate chip cookies don't taste as good as my mother's or because she happened to leave a light on in the house when she went to work that morning. The result is that I have to cook my own dinner, which is punishment enough, and that instead of being able to enjoy a night at home with a terrific woman I have to spend the evening trying to repair the damage my outburst has done.

The moral of the story is this: Don't let your emotions control you. Don't allow them to decide when, where, and how they will be expressed. Take control of them by recognizing their presence and by choosing a proper time and way to let them out.

How can we ventilate our emotions constructively? We might do it by running three miles or by lifting weights in order to release the day's built-up tensions. At times we might find it appropriate to cry. We may find it necessary to confront the person toward whom we feel angry. We may express our grief or our joy by praying out loud in a room all by ourselves. However we may choose to do it, and there are numerous constructive and acceptable means to employ, it is imperative that we do not allow our emotions to fester randomly inside of us. To do so can only hurt us.

While many Christians continue to live with the mistaken notion that a strong, mature person shouldn't need to express his hurts or pains, others believe that a mature Christian should be immune to hurt or doubt or grief and so should have no reason to be emotional. Yet those notions are simply not true.

There is no need to argue that Jesus Christ is the supreme example for the Christian. Jesus Christ is our God, our Saviour, Lord, and King. But Jesus also walked this earth as a man, and as a man He experienced all the emotions that we experience.

The Bible recounts for us three occasions on which Jesus cried. The first instance immediately follows the account of Christ's triumphal entry into Jerusalem, His grand entrance on Palm Sunday to the cheers and adulation of the crowds. But then we read: "And when He approached, He saw the city and wept over it" (Luke 19:41). The word *wept* in the Greek means that Jesus wailed bitterly, that He was deeply grieved. Why was He weeping? Because even though the people were acclaiming Him as their king, they were still blind to the truth. They didn't understand that He came to be king of their lives and not a king who would lead them in revolt against the oppression of Rome. Jesus responded to the blindness and neediness of the people of Jerusalem with sobs of grief. Strong men do cry.

The second occasion on which Jesus was moved to tears is in the familiar and moving account of the resurrection of Lazarus. Jesus arrived on the scene a few days after Lazarus had died and been buried. Mary and Martha complained that if only Jesus had come sooner he wouldn't have died at all. The account continues:

When Jesus therefore saw her [Mary] weeping, and the Jews who came with her, also weeping, He was deeply moved in spirit, and troubled; and said, "Where have you laid him?" They said to Him, "Lord, come and see." Jesus wept (John 11:33-35).

The words used to describe Jesus' reaction literally mean that He was enraged, violently angry, and deeply grieved.

Why? Because death is the enemy. Death is a tool of Satan. It is never a good—it is always an evil.

A few years ago Dr. Garth Rosell, now Dean of Gordon-Conwell Seminary, related to an audience his experience with grief on the death of his mother-in-law. She had been a very active and influential Christian, and died very suddenly. At her funeral a number of well-meaning friends attempted to comfort Dr. Rosell by saying, "Isn't it good that God has taken her home!" Garth's response was quite mixed. He agreed that his mother-in-law was in a much better world now that she was with the Lord. But Garth shared that his deeper feeling was one of anger and a powerful sense of loss because death is not a good. It came into our world as the result of mankind's sin and it is now in the arsenal of Satan (Heb. 2:14).

The source of Jesus' anger and deep pain was not only that He had lost a good friend, but also that death had claimed another victory, though only a temporary one. Death is a product of the fall of mankind. Not only do we hate death, but God hates it too. Death is one of Satan's weapons in his battle against God. It is our enemy.

Because death is an evil, because it is our enemy, it is appropriate to grieve when a loved one dies, even though we understand that they have only gone on to live in a better world. Edith Schaeffer asserts:

> Weeping is not something which Christians are not supposed to do or to feel. . . . Christians are behaving as God describes in His Word as "natural" when they weep as a result of death. It is God who will wipe away all tears—not another human being (*Affliction*, p. 21).

The third occasion on which Jesus wept was in the Garden of Gethsemane. It was there that Jesus prayed that God might, if possible, provide another means of saving mankind instead of through His agony on the cross. In Hebrews 5:7 we read, "In the days of His flesh, Jesus offered up prayers and supplications, with loud cries and tears, to Him who was able to save Him from death" (RSV). Why did Jesus cry in the Garden?

Because He was facing a personal crisis, and the same fears and doubts that overwhelm us at such times overwhelmed Him.

When we find ourselves confronted with the pain that persists, with a gnawing, aggravating irritation that just won't go away, we are certain to be flooded with a variety of powerful emotions. We may deny what is happening to us. We may be angry. We may become depressed. But whatever emotions come, we needn't be afraid of them nor resist them. Instead we should take them to God and ask Him to help us ventilate them in a careful, constructive, and acceptable way. God gave us our emotions—all of them. They are a precious gift. They each have their proper time, place, and means of expression. Before your emotions take control of you, take control of them by expressing them constructively.

God's Gift—People

While it is important to express our emotions and to vent our feelings, doing so is only the first step. The second step we can take, when we find ourselves paralyzed by pain, is to *lean on other people.*

Just as we sometimes find it difficult to ventilate our emotions, so we may find it difficult to go to another person for help. We don't like to admit that there are times in our lives when life becomes more than we can handle on our own, that we are facing a situation that is too much for us.

One of God's gifts to us, whether we are in pain or not, is His people, the body of Christ. Through His own people God is able to put His arm around our shoulder, to give us words of comfort, to provide a listening ear. No matter what situation we are in, God has prepared someone to be His agent of comfort. Paul assured us of this:

Blessed be the God and Father of our Lord Jesus Christ, the Father of mercies and God of all comfort, who comforts us in all our affliction so that we may be able to comfort those who are in any affliction with the comfort with which we ourselves are comforted by God (2 Cor. 1:3-4).

Someone somewhere has gone through an experience similar to yours and has been sustained and encouraged by the comfort of God. Moreover, that person has been prepared by God so that he can share God's comfort with you.

Joni Eareckson, whose life message has been a powerful source of comfort to many, learned this truth. Out of the grief and pain she has experienced in being a quadriplegic since 17, God has taught her numerous invaluable lessons. Here is one she shares in her book *A Step Further*:

We should never be alone when we suffer. I don't mean never for a minute, or that we must not live in an apartment by ourselves. But we should never build a self-imposed wall around us that allows absolutely no one inside to see what we're going through and to hurt with our hurts. God never intended that we shoulder the load of suffering by ourselves (Zondervan, p. 97).

One of the most intriguing sights in all the world is the sight of a flock of migrating geese flying along in their huge V-shaped formation. Scientists tell us that the weaker and injured geese fly in the rear of the formation so they can simply glide along in the stream created by the rest of the geese. The strongest geese are the ones who have the arduous task of breaking the air current and leading the way.

But the lead geese don't remain in front for the whole flight. They aren't strong enough to fly against the wind continually. From time to time they will fall back in the flock and let some of the other geese take the lead so that they can recuperate and regain their strength.

No matter how strong we are, there are times in our lives when we are unable to handle all the pressure and stress that weigh so heavily on us. For those times, God has given us a gift—His people. Through individuals God has especially prepared, God is able to reach out to us in a tangible way to give us comfort, hope, and strength.

God's Gift—Grace

The third step we can take in times of crisis is to *put our hope in God*. There are times when we've cried our eyes out and have been comforted by our friends, and yet still hurt so much that we just want to die. At those times God beckons us to turn to Him, to the source of all comfort, to place our trust and our hope completely in Him.

When the Apostle Paul was overwhelmed with persistent pain, he called out to God for healing. He described his pain as a "thorn in the flesh" that constantly harassed him. Because the pain persisted, Paul persisted in his pleas to God to remove the source of his pain, to heal his wound, to deliver him from his circumstances. Three times he approached God. I am sure he prayed with absolute faith that God could heal him. But three times God said no.

God had another gift for Paul that was even better than healing. The gift was God's grace: "'My grace is sufficient for you, for power is perfected in weakness.' Most gladly, therefore, I will rather boast about my weaknesses, that the power of Christ may dwell in me" (2 Cor. 12:9).

God promised Paul, as He promises us, that if we put our trust in Him He will provide us with everything we need to endure, and to live above our source of pain. God's grace includes His power, His wisdom, His patience, His love, His joy, His hope, and every other resource we will need. His grace is sufficient for us, all we'll ever need. Even if we have lost our limbs, our job, our home, or our spouse, His grace is more than enough to compensate that loss.

In 1 Corinthians 10:13 we read a similar promise. While the word *temptation* in this verse is usually taken to mean "an enticement to sin," its broader meaning in the Greek is that of a trial or testing of any kind. It can be a trial through an enticement to sin or it can be a trial through a difficult or disastrous circumstance. The promise God gives is this: "No temptation has overtaken you that is not common to man. God is faithful, and He will not let you be tempted beyond your strength, but with the temptation will also provide the way of escape, that you may be able to endure it" (RSV). God will never allow more pain than we can handle to come into our lives. He will provide us with every resource we need in order to live abundantly even in our pain.

In His grace and His love God sometimes allows us to understand why we are made to suffer such pain. Sometimes He pulls back the curtains of heaven just a bit to give us a glimpse of understanding, a peek at the positive results there will be because of what we are enduring. Sometimes God speaks to us most clearly about His love for us and the direction He wants our lives to take through our pain. C.S. Lewis once wrote, "God whispers to us in our pleasure, speaks in our conscience, but shouts in our pain: it is His megaphone to rouse a deaf world."

God can use our bruises. He can use them to speak to us, and He can use them to reveal His power to an unbelieving world as we respond to a shattering situation with peace, joy, and hope. He can use them to change us, to motivate us, to guide us. In fact, pain is one of God's gifts to us!

Dr. Paul Brand has written in his book *Fearfully and Wonderfully Made* that lepers suffer primarily from a loss of the sense of pain. As the leper gradually loses the sense of pain he tends to misuse those body parts most dependent on pain for protection, such as the feet and the hands. God has given us pain as a gift to protect us from something more harmful. The burnt finger warns us not to stick our hand in the fire. Falling off a short ladder teaches us to be careful when climbing higher structures. Pain is a gift to protect us from more serious harm.

Sometimes God uses our bruises, our pain, to warn us of some greater danger. God has used pain in the lives of many of His people to protect them from the danger of selfishness, or the danger of self-reliance, or the danger of greed. While the pain we experience now seems quite awful, in truth it is a gift of God to deliver us from a far worse fate that awaits the ungodly who ignore God—hell.

But sometimes God chooses not to pull back the curtains. Sometimes we have no inkling at all of why God has allowed such a horrible, wretched thing to take place in our lives. It is then, more than ever, that we must remember to *put our hope in God*. The Bible challenges us to believe and trust God even when we don't understand the whys, even when what has happened to us seems absurd and pointless. The suffering Job endured seemed quite meaningless to him. His family, his possessions, and his health were all wrenched away from him for no apparent reason. In his misery and bewilderment he cried out, "Why God? What purpose does this serve? What have I done to deserve this?"

Did God give Job an answer? Did He ever explain to him that he was part of a larger battle in the heavens between God and Satan? No, God never explained His reasons. But Job continued to trust God, to put his hope in his Creator. He trusted because even though he didn't know why he was suffering, he knew why he could trust the God who knows the whys. In the words of Os Guinness, "We can always have sure and sufficient reasons for knowing why we can trust God, but we cannot always know what God is doing and why" (*In Two Minds*, InterVarsity, p. 254).

There is no complete answer to the question of why you or I or our families are sometimes subjected to such intense suffering, such exasperating injustice, such measureless misery. God provides us with some pieces of the puzzle, but only in heaven will all the pieces be put together to form a meaningful picture. Until then we, like countless Christians who have gone before us, must steadfastly persevere in putting our trust in the God who knows the whys.

When our desire for health, wholeness, and happiness is frustrated by persistent, nagging pain, where can we turn for help? Where? To God who is our help.

God's help comes in the form of three gifts: the gift of our emotions, the gift of His people, and the gift of His grace. He has given us our emotions to provide a release for the pain that would prevent us from experiencing the peace and joy that can be ours when His Spirit fills ours. He has given us His people, individuals who have been prepared by Him to be physical agents of His comfort, encouragement, and strength. He has given us His grace, the sum total of every good thing, of every needed resource, to enable us to live above our pain and to experience the life of abundance that can't be limited by even the worst affliction. There is no night so dark that the stars do not still shine, no hole so deep that God's grace is not deeper still. When the pain persists, so does God's grace.

10

Locked in a Room With Open Doors

On November 23, 1970 a large Russian ship linked with a much smaller U.S. Coast Guard vessel for the purpose of conducting talks between the U.S. and the U.S.S.R. regarding international fishing regulations. As the talks drew to a close Simas Kudirka, a Lithuanian sailor with 20 years of experience, made a flying leap from his mother ship to the Coast Guard vessel, risking his life and leaving behind the wife and child he loved so much. When asked by the Americans why he defected, he replied, "Freedom."

But instead of freedom Simas Kudirka was to face three years in prison. In a series of political maneuvers, the U.S. was forced to return Kudirka to the Russians who convicted him of treason and sentenced him to Siberia. He spent the next three years locked behind bars, away from his family and subjected to the bitter cold of Siberian winters. Through the persistent efforts of friends inside the United States, Simas Kudirka and his family were to taste freedom for the first time on November 23, 1974, four years after he had jumped from the Russian ship. Today Simas Kudirka lives as a free man.

At the age of 29, Viktor Belenko had it all. Because he was a fighter pilot and at the top of his class, the Communist Party rewarded him with many luxuries never accorded to most other Russians. While Soviet doctors earn 120 rubles per month, Belenko earned 300 rubles per month. While the average Soviet couple waits seven to eight years to be able to rent an apartment, Belenko and his wife were issued an apartment immediately. Though meat and vegetables are often unavailable and food lines are extremely long, Belenko was given four free meals a day every day of the year. Because of his achievements and his dedication Belenko was even used in advertisements to depict the ideal Communist of the future.

But Belenko still lacked one thing—freedom. On September 6, 1976, while flying maneuvers in the sophisticated MiG-25, Viktor Belenko broke off from his flight pattern and landed in Japan where he asked for asylum in the United States. Today Viktor Belenko lives as a free man ("MiG Pilot," John Barron, *Reader's Digest*, January 1980, p. 188).

From 1965—1973 Vice Admiral James B. Stockdale sat chained in a cell 10 feet long and 4 feet wide as a Vietnamese prisoner of war. Many of his days were spent in interrogation as the Communists used every possible means of torture to break him down. Much of his time was spent in solitary confinement. Finally, after eight years in prison, Vice Admiral James Stockdale was released. He lives today as a free man.

The desire to be free is a driving force in the life of every human being. God has built that need into us. We want to be free to choose who we will spend our lives with. We want to be free to pursue our own aspirations and goals instead of goals set for us by someone else. Perhaps the value Americans exalt more highly than any other is freedom. To be American is to cherish freedom as one cherishes his own child.

Locked in a Room With Open Doors

Yet the frustrating reality for many people is that they are not free. Their prison is not one with steel bars and armed guards. Instead of being locked in a cage or a cell with the doors tightly bolted, they are confined in a room with open doors.

Ernest Campbell, former pastor of New York's Riverside Church, told of a book he read while vacationing in a rustic cottage one summer. One chapter begins with these words:

In a family of my acquaintance were two brothers, the younger of whom had a dread of open doors. The older one became impatient, as older brothers will be, and wanting to break him of his habit, he threatened: "One day I will lock you up in a room with all the doors open."

Most of us are of the firm opinion that the reason we aren't experiencing the abundant life we desire is because the doors are closed to us. The door to that job we really want is closed by our lack of education or by our sex or race. The door to the home we'd like to buy is closed by skyrocketing interest rates or the substantial debts we have already accrued. The door to exuberant health is closed by a crippling disease or the steady accumulation of years. And try as we might, those doors won't be opened. We've used keys and crowbars. We've knocked politely and we've pounded vigorously. But despite our best efforts, happiness and abundance and prosperity have remained securely locked up behind closed doors.

Yet more often than not, the door to happiness and abundance and prosperity is wide open! We aren't limited or restrained by closed doors, but by our own inability to walk through the open ones. We find ourselves face to face with an open door, an open opportunity, an open road to the fulfillment of our dreams. Yet our feet remain riveted to the floor like magnets to a steel girder.

There is a story of a sailor in ancient times who was bound by choice to a 45-pound bronze statue of the goddess Diana. She was his good luck charm, his savior, and he never traveled without her. On one trip he was tossed overboard by the rough seas. He thought it fortunate that his statue was thrown over with him. As he bobbed up and down in the middle of the Mediterranean, he clung tenaciously to the statue, all the while rubbing its head and trying frantically to recall some incantation that would move Diana to rescue him. But the statue gave him no help, and in time the 45-pound weight became an unbearable drag. What he thought was his savior had become his enemy. He had locked himself in a room with open doors (W. Ross Foley, *You Can Win Over Weariness*, Regal, p. 30).

While vacationing on the Queen Elizabeth as it cruised in the waters of the Atlantic, a pastor found himself unable to sleep and went up on deck. There he met a Yugoslavian man en route to his homeland. The pastor asked the Yugoslav how he liked the trip, and in German the man replied that he did not like it at all because he was bored.

This puzzled the pastor, since there was so much on board to do: movies, a library, parties, shuffleboard, and numerous other forms of entertainment. When he mentioned those activities he noticed that his fellow passenger looked very surprised. He didn't realize he could do all those things—he thought the ticket he bought only entitled him to a bed and meals! With no end of entertainment available, this man was bored. Why? Because he had locked himself in a room with open doors!

The reality for most of us is that we are immobilized and restricted not so much by *external* obstacles as by *internal* barriers. We yearn for wholeness, for freedom, for joy, for power, for love, and for intimacy. But while the doors to all of those experiences are wide open, we find ourselves paralyzed by our own weaknesses and fears, by our memories, our pride, and our sin.

When our desire for freedom is frustrated not by external obstacles but by our own inadequacies, where can we turn? How can we be released from our self-made prisons? Where can we find the strength to boldly break loose of the intangible chains that shackle us and to run through the doors God has already opened for us?

New Legs for the Paralytic

The way to gain freedom from this particular frustration is illustrated for us in the story of Jesus' healing of the paralytic. It shows us what true freedom is and how we can be set free by the miraculous healing power of Jesus Christ. Through the power of God the weak legs of the paralytic were made new and whole. Through the power of God, the fears and memories and sin that paralyze us and keep us locked in a room with open doors can also be healed. Jesus Christ can set us free!

This story is the first of five consecutive passages in Luke dealing with the conflicts that Jesus had with the Pharisees and the elders. The word about Jesus' startling sermons and His amazing power to heal had spread like a fire in a dry forest, and more and more people were eager to see for themselves just what He could do. Not only the common people were curious about Jesus, but now even the elite of the religious hierarchy had come to observe Him firsthand. Here is the story as Luke tells it.

On one of those days, as He was teaching, there were Pharisees and teachers of the law sitting by, who had come from every village of Galilee and Judea and from Jerusalem; and the power of the Lord was with Him to heal. And behold, men were bringing on a bed a man who was paralyzed, and they sought to bring him in and lay him before Jesus; but finding no way to bring him in, because of the crowd, they went up on the roof and let him down with his bed through the tiles into the midst before Jesus. And when He saw their faith He said, "Man, your sins are forgiven you." And the scribes and the Pharisees began to question, saying, "Who is this that speaks blasphemies? Who can forgive sins but God only?" When Jesus perceived their questionings, He answered them, "Why do you question in your hearts? Which is easier, to say, 'Your sins are forgiven you,' or to say 'Rise and walk'? But that you may know that the Son of man has authority on earth to forgive sins"—He said to the man who was paralyzed—"I say to you, rise, take up your bed and go home." And immediately he rose before them, and took up that on which he lay, and went home, glorifying God. And amazement seized them all, and they glorified God and were filled with awe, saying, "We have seen strange things today" (Luke 5:17-26, RSV).

Each of the major characters in this episode has a unique perspective to offer us. The Pharisees and the teachers were the objective onlookers who came to watch Jesus in action. They might have even been amused by all the fuss being made over this Galilean. But their amusement quickly turned to anger when they heard what Jesus said to the paralytic. They had heard that this Jesus possessed a remarkable power to heal. They were almost ready to concede that He was a charismatic teacher, even a person worthy of their coveted stamp of approval. But what audacity to actually suggest that He could forgive the paralytic's sins! Was He inferring that He was God? God alone can forgive sins, and a person wouldn't have to be very intelligent to see that this man was not God!

The four friends of the paralytic had a different perspective. They loved their friend dearly and were willing to do anything to help him. They had lugged him for some distance to meet Jesus, but when they arrived they found it impossible to even get near because of the crush of people.

But they weren't about to be stopped now! They had learned to see their problems as possibilities, their obstacles as opportunities. They discovered that there was a way to get to Jesus—through the roof! Hurriedly they yanked up the tiles and scratched away the mud and straw to make an opening in the roof right above Jesus. They weren't too concerned with what other people thought of their bold actions. They didn't care if they offended some people—they were going to help their friend, and nothing was going to stop them!

Then there was the perspective of the paralytic. We have no idea of his age or of how long he had been paralyzed. We don't know what caused his paralysis. But we can imagine the excitement he must have felt when his friends told him they were going to take him to see Jesus, a man said to be able to heal paralytics! Just think—a chance to walk again, to run, to live normally. He wouldn't need to depend on his friends to carry him places, to bring him food, to wait on him. He could finally be free of the pallet that made his bones and muscles ache so. Imagine the wild beating of his heart as his friends lowered him down through the roof and placed him squarely in front of Jesus.

Silence descended on the crowd like a blanket of snow covering a barren hillside. All eyes were focused on Jesus and the helpless paralytic lying at His feet. Could Jesus really heal this man? What an extraordinary happening it would be! Wait—quiet! Jesus was about to speak.

"Man, your sins are forgiven you!"

What did He say? Did we hear wrong? Did He tell the man that his sins are forgiven? Why would He say such an absurd thing? The crowd buzzed with bewilderment. The Pharisees were livid with rage!

But the paralytic understood. He knew that his greatest problem wasn't his physical paralysis but his inner paralysis. His lame legs weren't keeping him from abundant life. He had locked himself out by his sin. He had been locked in a room with open doors. But now, now he would be free. Whether he was healed was no longer the main issue, because he had already been released from his internal chains, and been given the freedom to live the abundant life in all its fullness.

Jesus looked up from the paralytic and gazed intently at the confused and angry sea of faces surrounding Him.

"Why do you question in your hearts? Which is easier, to say 'Your sins are forgiven you,' or to say 'Rise and walk'?"

Then Jesus turned back to the paralytic and in a voice resonating with authority and compassion, He said, "Rise, take up your bed and go home." Without hesitation the paralytic leaped to his feet! He was free to walk, to dance, to run through the fields! And even more important, he knew he was free inside from his sin, from its guilt and penalty, and its power to deprive him of life in its fullness. The doors had been opened and he had been set loose.

The Chains of the Past

Like the paralytic, the greatest restrictions on our freedom are not the closed doors of circumstances, but internal obstacles. What are some of these barriers to freedom? What prevents us from experiencing life as God meant it to be lived?

● While there are many barriers to our freedom, I would like to focus on three that appear to me to be the most difficult to overcome. The first obstacle that many of us face is *memories*. We are paralyzed by our past. We find ourselves chained by our hurts, by the tragedies that victimized us years ago but which continue to haunt us.

Twenty-year-old Patricia Hearst heard a knock at the door and casually got up to answer it. The men she met when she opened the door that fateful day belonged to the Symbionese Liberation Army and were to turn her life into a nightmare. Her kidnappers abused her physically, "brainwashed" her, and before long Patty Hearst had been transformed into a bank robber wanted by the FBI.

The terror and trauma that Patty Hearst and her family were subjected to is over. Life has returned to normal for them. Patty Hearst is happily married to Bernie Shaw, one of her former bodyguards. They have bought a new home in Northern California.

Yet Patty Hearst is still not free. In her autobiography *Every Secret Thing* (Doubleday and Company), she reveals that she lives "behind locked doors in a Spanish-style house equipped with the best electronic security system available." She reports that her house is surrounded by a thick wall secured by an iron gate, that she is guarded by two German shepherds, and that she has been trained in the use of certain weapons she has acquired to defend herself. She has been described by friends as eager to move on and to live an ordinary life, but unable to keep from looking over her shoulder. The past continues to grip Patty Hearst like a parasite extorting its host. It will not permit her to be free.

Mary Vincent is a prisoner in the same cell as Patty Hearst. In September of 1978 Mary was picked up while hitchhiking from Berkeley to Los Angeles. Before the evening was over she had been stripped, attacked, and her arms had been chopped off. By the time she was brought to a hospital in Modesto, she had lost six pints of blood. Miraculously, Mary Vincent survived. Yet she is still not free:

The scars remain. The prosthetic arms are constant re- minders of the gruesome attack. Her nightmares are even more frightening.

She wakes up in the middle of the night, her face sweating profusely, the pillow soaking wet, and her eyes filled with tears. Each time, the nightmares start out dif- ferently but the ending is always the same—a replay of the attack.

In the last year and a half, she has had only two pleasant dreams. She used to run frantically in her sleep, knocking over tables and chairs and running into walls. The violent nightmares have stopped, but the bad dreams remain. . . .

Mary still holds feelings of contempt for her attacker. It is likely she always will. Her parents fear she will hold a lifetime of hatred in her heart. (Glenn Bunting, "Daunt- less Spirit Conquers Horror," San Jose *Mercury News*, March 23, 1980).

While we may have never experienced the horrifying trau- mas of a Patty Hearst or a Mary Vincent, all of us have skeletons in our past that we'd rather keep locked up in the closet. Despite our best efforts, though, those skeletons man- age to sneak out of hiding from time to time to claim posses- sion of our minds and our lives.

But it needn't be that way. Jesus Christ has opened the door for us by His death and resurrection. God has promised to give us His Holy Spirit to heal our memories and to give us power to overcome our fear and bitterness, our guilt and grief.

Dennis Whitman is an intern at Teen Challenge in San Francisco. Each week, besides counseling drug-dependent juveniles, he goes into area prisons to share the Gospel in city jails. But Dennis' experience with drugs and jails is not confined to counseling. Just a few years ago he was a frequent user of marijuana, amphetamines, barbiturates, and LSD. In 1969 he was arrested for selling LSD and spent the next five years in prison. On release from prison he immediately made his way back into the drug world and began to experiment with PCP, otherwise known as "angel dust." Two days after he had gone on a PCP high he killed his own brother in a fit of insanity, and was sent back to prison on a charge of involuntary manslaughter.

But something significant happened to Dennis Whitman while he was locked up in San Quentin prison. A fellow prisoner gave him a Bible and told him about the freedom he could have through a relationship with Jesus Christ. Here's how Dennis Whitman describes what happened next:

When my friend came back I was ready to accept Jesus Christ into my life. That was the best decision I ever made. Since that day I haven't been the same! For two years I served the Lord while in prison. I became a deacon in the prison church and also was the chairman of a group called Free Cons in Christ. . . . God has constantly given me back the years I had lost. . . . God set me free from a terrible lifestyle and has made a new creature out of me. I praise God for showing me what life is all about ("My Search For Life," Dennis Whitman, Teen Challenge *Newsletter*).

God can heal our memories. He can give us back the years we thought we had lost. He can deliver us from our fears, our guilt, our hate, our anger, and our nightmares. He can make us into new creatures. He can fill our lives with peace, with confidence, and with a new capacity to love. God can free us from our past.

● A second cause of internal paralysis is *pride*. As Americans we are a very independent sort of people. We pride ourselves on being able to do things in our own way without anyone's help. We don't want to let anyone know that we have hurts and sometimes need help.

After living as a bachelor for seven years, I felt rather proud of how well I could take care of myself. I could clean house, wash and iron my clothes, sew, handle my finances, and cook well enough to keep from starving. I used to bristle whenever any well-meaning individual would suggest that what I really needed was to marry some capable woman who would take care of me. My response came quickly and with emotion: "I don't need anyone to take care of me! I can take care of myself."

There are many of us who don't like to admit that we could ever use someone else's help. After my grandfather had his first in a series of strokes, it became necessary for people to help him with even routine tasks. He needed to be shaved and helped in getting dressed. After a long time he came to accept his restrictions, but his initial reaction was that of an independent, obstinate Norwegian: "No, Sir!" which being interpreted means, "Not on your life, Buckwheat!"

What would have happened if the paralytic had been too proud to let his friends help him, if he had played the role of the independent, rugged individual who could make it on his own? He would never have been healed! He needed his friends. He was paralyzed without them, but with their help he was able to become a whole, healthy, free person.

One of the causes of our spiritual and emotional paralysis is that we are too independent to let other people know about our hurts and needs, too proud to let them help us. We are paralyzed, chained by our pride. But it needn't be that way, for the doors are open. Like the paralytic we can be free if we will only be willing to put our faith and our trust in the people around us and let them help us in our struggles. God uses people to set us free, just as He sent four very caring, daring friends to help the paralytic find freedom.

● A third cause of internal paralysis is *unbelief.* The door to a supernatural life may be open to us, but we can't bring ourselves to believe it is possible.

One of the most endearing characters in the 1980 blockbuster movie, *The Empire Strikes Back,* is the elfin wizard Yoda. Yoda is the creature who for centuries has trained warriors to be Jedi Knights by teaching them how to make use of the power of the Force. His project in this story is to train Luke Skywalker in the use of the Force. Gradually the impatient Luke learns to use the Force to move rocks and levitate other small objects. Yet when his final test is given, Luke fails. Yoda instructs Luke to raise his spaceship, which is mired in the swamp, through the concentration of his will. When Luke is unable to do so, Yoda steps in to show him how it's done. After watching in amazement as Yoda levitates the ship to dry land, Luke exclaims, "I don't believe it." Returns Yoda: "That's why you failed."

When did Jesus inform the paralytic that his sins were forgiven? "When He saw their faith." Faith is the key by which our internal prison doors are opened and our spirits set free! Without faith we are exiled to live forever locked in a room with open doors. With it, all things are possible to us!

What is it that is paralyzing you right now? What is keeping you from experiencing life in its fullness? Is it your painful past? Is it fear? Is it pride? Is it unbelief? Is it guilt or confusion or bitterness? Whatever it is, the message of the Gospel of Jesus Christ is that the door is already open. God can give new legs to the paralytic, new hope to the discouraged, new strength to the weak. He can set you free of whatever it is that binds you and restrains you. The door to life, the door to freedom, the door to power and purpose and peace is wide open. The next step is yours. Rise up and live!

11

When There's No Way Out

For two summers I worked as the director of the junior high program at Northern Pines, a family camp in Lake Geneva, Wisconsin. As the director and senior counselor I became the object of every conceivable prank junior highers are capable of, including innovations such as putting cereal and dry pancakes in my bed, hiding an alarm clock underneath my mattress set to go off at 2:00 A.M., and pouring garbage baskets full of cold water on my head from the roof of the dormitory.

Naturally, such antisocial behavior cannot go undisciplined, and we counselors devised means of retribution which we called "99" and "pink belly." Lest the reader consider these means of discipline a bit barbaric, let me remind you of the severity of the crime—climbing in bed with pancakes and bran flakes is no joy. The means of discipline called "99" consists of 99 very moderate but well-placed blows to the victim's sternum with one's knuckle. "Pink belly" is the process of turning the victim's stomach pink by continual and rapid slaps of the counselor's hands. Of the two we found pink belly to be the more effective deterrent to repeated crimes.

On the last night of camp, the counselors usually allow the kids to stay up a bit later, to make noise and enjoy themselves.

Being the very generous and noble director that I was, I told my other counselors to go out and relax for a while, assuring them that I would be able to handle the kids myself until I needed help to get everyone to bed.

After the other counselors left, I went into the lounge where most of the kids were. One of the girls offered to give me a backrub, which I found hard to refuse, and so I lay down on my stomach while she and another girl began to massage my back. I soon discovered that the backrub was only a scheme to get me to take my shirt off. While I lay there relaxed, suddenly a horde of vengeful, bloodthirsty junior highers descended on me like a swarm of mosquitoes and with great delight and enthusiasm proceeded to administer my punishment—the dreaded pink belly! I was outnumbered fifty to one and the other counselors were too far away to hear me. My time had come, and there was no way out!

We all face frustrations on a daily basis. Often our problems are of the short-term variety and are more of a nuisance than anything else. The car breaks down on the freeway and we're late for an appointment. The dog, after 12 years of obediently abstaining from any extracurricular activities on the carpeting, is suddenly overcome with senility and has a major accident in the living room, just 15 minutes before the pastor is due to call on you. Sometimes the frustrations we face are of a bit greater magnitude, such as how to scrape up enough money to pay next month's rent, or how to resolve a conflict that is threatening the stability of marriage.

Yet we can do something about most of the frustrations we face. We can take concrete action to overcome whatever hurdle is in our way. We can get our car fixed, we can clean up the mess on the rug and put the dog in a nursing home, we can get a loan or a new job, we can enter marriage counseling or propose a compromise to solve our problems. These are the frustrations that we are able to handle using our own ingenuity, resources, and courage.

But there is another variety of frustration that on occasion afflicts each of us, the kind we can't do anything about, for no amount of effort or creativity or fortitude is going to bail us out. It is the frustration for which there is no answer, no escape.

Fourteen-year-old Mary and Susan were quite excited to have boyfriends who showered them with compliments and affection. But their boyfriends also happened to have addictive and expensive drug habits. Within a short time, their "boyfriends" became their pimps, as Mary and Susan were forced into prostitution to support the drug habits. The girls desperately wanted to get out of prostitution, but feared that contracts would be put out on their lives if they tried to escape. Fourteen years old—and no way out ("Teen-Ageism," Tom Alexander, Teen Challenge *Newsletter*).

A 22-year-old triplegic wrote Joni Eareckson the following letter:

This (the triplegia) happened to me in 1968 after my mother hit me on the head. It took six surgeries to save me. I was at Cook County Hospital for one year. Then I was sent to the Rehabilitation Institute of Chicago for a year and a half. Then I went to Grant Hospital for surgery on my arms and legs.

I have been back to the Rehabilitation Institute eight times. So far I have had 22 surgeries. I am still the same. I am in a chair. I have no family and take care of myself. . . . I don't have a lot of faith in God. I feel I cannot overcome this (Joni Eareckson and Steve Estes: *A Step Further*, Zondervan, pp. 163-164).

What happens to a person who is consistently frustrated, who finds himself trapped by circumstances that he can't change? One of the theories about the causes of schizophrenia is called the "double bind theory." The theory holds that some people become schizophrenic when confronted by a situation in which there is no way out, where they are frustrated whichever way they turn.

To substantiate this theory psychologists placed a rat in a cage with an air hose directly behind it. The only way of escape for the rat when the air hose went into operation was a circular opening at the end of the cage. The first time the air hose blasted the rat it simply ran through the opening to safety. The second time the rat again ran through the opening, but this time the researchers had arranged the cage so that when the rat ran through the opening he would suddenly fall 12 feet. Now there was no way out for the rat. He was in a double bind with the air hose behind him and a 12-foot drop in front of him. The next time the rat was placed in the cage with the air hose he again ran through the opening and fell 12 feet to a painful landing. But this time after the fall the rat limped into the corner, urinated, and then promptly went into a state of catatonic schizophrenia.

What do we do when there's no way out? When we face a frustration that is bigger than we are and we don't know which way to turn, is there anything more we can do besides cry, complain, or be cynical?

The good news of the Gospel is that with God there is always a way out, that God never closes a door without opening a window. Over 2,500 years ago one of God's special people, a king by the name of Jehoshaphat, was faced with a situation in which there was no way out. Through his story we will discover God's method of freeing us from those special frustrations for which there seems to be no answer. Let's begin by looking at Jehoshaphat's problem.

The Problem

Jehoshaphat was one of the kings of ancient Judah. According to history Israel was divided into two kingdoms following the reigns of King David and his son, King Solomon. Jereboam became the first king of the Northern Kingdom known as Israel, and Rehoboam became the first king of the Southern Kingdom, known as Judah. Jehoshaphat was the fourth king of Judah, inheriting the throne from his father Asa.

A quick reading of the four books of Kings and Chronicles will reveal that most of the rulers of the two ancient countries were greedy, selfish, and idolatrous. But Jehoshaphat was a godly king who ruled with justice and compassion. He led the people into the worship of God rather than to worship the many popular false gods. Because of his righteous life and rule, God blessed Jehoshaphat's reign with prosperity and peace.

But one day Jehoshaphat found himself face to face with a frustration unlike any he had ever confronted before. Three of Judah's fiercest enemies—Ammon, Moab, and Edom—had joined together to attack Judah. After he learned about the situation, Jehoshaphat realized that he was in a heap of trouble. Notice his assessment of the problem:

And now behold, the men of Ammon and Moab and Mount Seir, whom Thou wouldest not let Israel invade when they came from the land of Egypt, and whom they avoided and did not destroy—behold, they reward us by coming to drive us out of Thy possession, which Thou hast given us to inherit. O our God, wilt Thou not execute judgment upon them? For we are powerless against this great multitude that is coming against us. We do not know what to do" (2 Chron. 20:10-12, RSV).

Jehoshaphat was badly outnumbered by the combined forces of the enemies. Surrender wasn't a feasible alternative because of the character of his opponents. Once before the Ammonites had surrounded Israel and had offered these generous terms of peace: "If you surrender, we will only gouge out your right eyes. If you don't surrender, we will massacre you" (1 Sam. 11). Jehoshaphat was in a double bind. He was powerless to defend his people and his land. He was trapped in his own city by a multitude of merciless marauders. There was simply no way out.

That was Jehoshaphat's problem. But what situations do we face from which there appears to be no way out?

Almost everyone at some point reaches a dead end. The mother of five runs herself into complete exhaustion, trying to take care of the needs of her kids, make ends meet on a tight budget, and cope with a husband who won't lift a finger to help around the house. She feels trapped by demanding kids, an unsympathetic husband, and inadequate funds. She gets no time off, little sleep, no sick days or mental health days, no chance to meet interesting people. She sees no way out.

The person who grew up in the ghetto quit school in order to get a job. He works ten hours a day six days a week just to make ends meet, and he's bored to tears with his job. Yet because he isn't qualified for other than a menial job, he knows he won't get out of the factory for the rest of his working life. He feels trapped in a job he hates and sees no hope of change.

The elderly couple living in the high-rise apartment have no family, no friends, no way to socialize. Both of them are in poor health, so they sit day after day and wait out their lives. There's nothing they can do to alter their situation.

A 25-year-old woman went to the newspaper office one day to divulge the story of her traumatic childhood, in hopes that she might make more people aware of the magnitude of the problem of incest. She told how from the time she was eight years old her father would sneak into her bedroom and use her physically. No amount of crying or screaming would discourage him. Her mother wouldn't believe her and her father denied everything she said. She tried running away, she tried drugs, and even suicide. But each time she left home, well-meaning people would bring her back. There was no escape for her until she was old enough to move away from home.

At some time or another all of us find ourselves feeling confused, frustrated, and helpless. What do we do when there's no way out?

The Perspective

Jehoshaphat found himself in a situation from which there was no escape, and he felt confused, frustrated, and helpless. But despite his frustration, Jehoshaphat had learned in his years of being a king that more important than anything else in a difficult situation is one's *perspective*. Jehoshaphat expressed his perspective when he said to God, "O our God, wilt Thou not judge them? For we are powerless before this great multitude who are coming against us; nor do we know what to do, but our eyes are upon Thee" (2 Chron. 20:12).

Even though Jehoshaphat had his back to the wall, he didn't fold. His perception of the situation was clear. He knew there was nothing he could do to change the circumstances or fight his way out. No amount of courage or creativity would rescue him from his dilemma. What was his perspective? "We do not know what to do, but our eyes are upon Thee."

Instead of focusing on the magnitude of his frustration, Jehoshaphat focused on the magnificence of his God! Most of us rivet our attention and energy on our frustration. We analyze, measure, worry, and become aggravated. Before long we find ourselves dominated by our frustration. Sleepless nights and unproductive days follow, one after the other. Even in our dreams, frustration confronts us. Finally we reach the conclusion that since the frustration is bigger than we are, there's no way out.

Jehoshaphat also concluded that the frustration was bigger than he was. There was no chance that his tiny nation could defeat the combined forces of Ammon, Edom, and Moab. He wasn't naive. He didn't close his eyes and hope the problem would go away. Instead he opened his eyes and saw the wider picture. He saw that behind his big problem was a bigger God! Somewhere Jehoshaphat had learned that God is greater than any circumstance, that He isn't limited by our inabilities, nor bewildered by our confusing situations. "We don't know what to do, but our eyes are upon Thee."

The psychologist Albert Ellis bases his theory of therapy, called Rational-Emotive Therapy, on a similar principle to the one Jehoshaphat employed. He noticed that the reason some people become debilitated by a certain event while others are able to overcome it is that their perspectives of the event differ. When one person is fired from his job he takes the perspective that he was fired because he is a terrible person who has nothing to contribute to the world and who might as well be dead. The person who takes that perspective becomes depressed, lonely, withdrawn, and even suicidal.

When the second person is fired from his job he takes a different perspective. He doesn't try to pretend that the situation isn't unfortunate or that he doesn't feel hurt and rejected. But he takes a positive approach. He realizes that there are a host of other jobs available, even though he might have to take further training or move to some other town to find them. Being fired from his job doesn't mean that he is a terrible, worthless person. He is a significant person, with certain deficiencies and limitations, like everyone else.

What are the results? The first person not only loses his job, but loses his friends as well, because of his negative, self-defeating attitude. He doesn't get another job because he has already concluded that he is worthless. The second individual does find another job and sees the whole process of being fired as a growing experience because it has forced him to reevaluate his abilities and goals. What's the difference between these two individuals? Perspective.

One of the most exhilarating experiences of my life was spending a week canoeing in the BWCA, the Boundary Waters Canoe Area. The BWCA is located on the Canadian—Minnesota border. The lake water is crystal clear and clean enough to drink. No motorboats are allowed. A person can canoe for days without seeing another canoe. At night the stars provide free entertainment. After spending all my life in the city, a week in the Boundary Waters was like a taste of heaven.

But canoeing the BWCA had its unpleasant side too. While the area largely consists of lakes, there are also numerous islands and stretches of wilderness separating the lakes. The only way to get from the end of one lake to the beginning of another is to portage. Strapping your backpack to your back, you balance the canoe on your head and shoulders and carry it through the brush to the next lake.

On the last day of our trip we encountered the longest portage of the week, about a mile and a half, and heavily overgrown with brush. The canoe never felt heavier than that last day. All I could think of was getting home, out of the mud and away from the bugs. When you are under a canoe it's difficult to see much of the scenery except for fallen trees, mud, and inclines. I began to wonder why I had even made the trip.

When we arrived back at the camp where we started from, we ran into a friend of ours who spent each of her summers in the BWCA as a canoe guide. When she asked how our trip went I seized the opportunity to detail for her how horrible it was to have to portage through a mile and a half of swamp, hills, brush, and bugs. After I finished my lengthy harangue, her eyes lit up like a pinball machine as she exclaimed, "Oh, I know that portage! Isn't it beautiful? That portage has the best scenery of any of the portages around here."

I was a bit surprised by her reaction and began to argue with her. "But Dana," I said, "how can you see any of the scenery when you have an 80-pound canoe on your back?"

Dana's reply taught me a lesson I'll never forget. She said, "Well, Craig, don't just look at your feet! Even under a canoe there are beautiful things to see, if you'll just look up a little bit."

Her words hit me like a lineman attacking a tackling dummy. I had spent a large part of my time in one of the few wilderness areas left in the country looking at something I see every day—my feet. But Dana saw all the beauty that wilderness has to offer because she forced herself to look up a little. What enabled her to see the beauty of that wilderness, while all I saw was mud? Her perspective!

While he was faced with what seemed like an impossible situation, Jehoshaphat had the wisdom to look up. He looked beyond the power of his enemies to focus on the power of his God. When Jehoshaphat took a fresh look at God, this was what he saw: "O Lord, the God of our fathers, art Thou not

God in the heavens? And art Thou not ruler over all the kingdoms of the nations? Power and might are in Thy hand so no one can stand against Thee" (v. 6).

No matter what our situation is, no matter how big our problem may be, as God's people we shouldn't let ourselves be blinded from seeing how great our God is. We need to keep our frustrations in perspective and see them as God sees them—as difficult, but never impossible.

The Promise

At this point someone might want to stop and argue: "It's fine to have that kind of perspective, but it won't change my situation! I'm still holed up in a corner with no way out!" That's true. Having the right perspective doesn't change the situation. But that's not the end of your story—or Jehoshaphat's:

> Meanwhile all the men of Judah stood before the Lord, with their little ones, their wives, and their children. And the Spirit of the Lord came upon Jahaziel. . . . And he said. . . . "Thus says the Lord to you, 'Fear not, and be not dismayed at this great multitude; for the battle is not yours but God's. . . . You will not need to fight in this battle; take your position, stand still, and see the victory of the Lord on your behalf, O Judah and Jerusalem'" (2 Chron. 20:13-17, RSV).

After Jehoshaphat turned to God in prayer and with the proper perspective, God gave him an astounding promise through the Prophet Jahaziel: "Jehoshaphat, I know there's nothing you can do. But it doesn't matter that you can't do anything to help yourself, because you don't have to! I'm going to fight this battle for you. You won't have to do anything!"

What great news! But what would have happened if Jehoshaphat had allowed himself to wallow in pity over his frustration instead of focusing on the greatness of God? He would never have heard God's promise! Many times we don't even hear God's promises to us because we aren't tuned in to Him. Because our perspective is all blurred we are looking for answers in the wrong places, focusing our attention and energy on the wrong things.

All the time God has some good news that He's trying to tell us. What is His promise to the paraplegic, to the single parent, to the lonely widow, to you and me? He promises us peace (John 14:27; Phil. 4:6-7); joy (John 15:11); wisdom and insight (John 14:26; James 1:5); power (John 14:12); forgiveness (1 John 1:9); grace to endure and overcome (2 Cor. 12:9-10); and eternal life (John 11:25-26). God promises to provide us with everything we need to live triumphantly in every situation, no matter how frustrating or confusing or horrible it seems to be. What is impossible for us is always possible with God!

The Power

What happened to Jehoshaphat? He gathered together all the people of Judah and took them out into the wilderness. When they arrived at their destination Jehoshaphat assured them that God was going to deliver them. Then, instead of sharpening their weapons or plotting strategy, they began to worship God!

And when they began to sing and praise, the Lord set an ambush against the men of Ammon, Moab, and Mount Seir, who had come against Judah, so that they were routed. For the men of Ammon and Moab rose against the inhabitants of Mount Seir, destroying them utterly, and when they had made an end of the inhabitants of Seir, they all helped to destroy one another (2 Chron. 20:22-23, RSV).

God came through on His promise. He fought the battle for them! He caused the allies who had joined together to fight Judah to turn on and destroy each other. God supported His promise with His power. The promises He makes to His people are not idle words. They are not given merely as a creed for positive thinkers so that we can go out and help ourselves. Each promise God makes is reinforced by His power to change, to heal, to comfort, and to give life.

On the night of December 7, 1946 when Stuart Luhan was awakened by loud noises in the hall of the hotel, he leaped out of bed and threw open the door to investigate. The smoke pouring through the corridors and the frantic shouts of the other hotel guests told him that the hotel was on fire.

Stuart Luhan ran back into his room and slammed the door to keep out the suffocating smoke. His fear intensified when he remembered that he was on the tenth floor of the hotel. He couldn't jump. He couldn't go back into the flaming hallway. There was no way out!

Then Stuart Luhan dropped to his knees and began to pray. After a few moments of fervent prayer, he noticed that the intense fear which had engulfed him was gone. He also sensed God instructing him to put on his clothes and to begin to make a rope out of the sheets, blankets, and bedspread. He did so even though he realized his rope couldn't possibly reach the safety of the street ten stories below.

After making the rope Mr. Luhan began to throw the rope out the window, but God seemed to be telling him to wait. Wait he did, though he began to wonder if he didn't have his signals crossed when he noticed the black smoke pouring under his door.

Finally the voice seemed to tell Mr. Luhan to go ahead. As he climbed out the window he spotted a fireman extending a ladder to the eighth floor, which was as far as it would reach, yet it was still one room to the right and a bit short of where Mr. Luhan's rope was. With a herculean effort, Stuart managed to swing over to the fireman and drop into his arms.

When he looked back at his rope he realized why he had been told to wait before throwing it out. His rope of sheets and blankets had quickly been gobbled up by the flames snaking out of the windows. Had he thrown out the rope when he first wanted to, it would have burned before the fireman had a chance to reach him (Catherine Marshall, *Beyond Ourselves*, McGraw-Hill, pp. 137-139).

With God there is always a way out. God never closes a door without opening a window. But whether we see the window depends on our perspective. When you're trapped in a corner with no way out, look up! God has a window opened just for you!

12

You Have To Get Out of the Boat

A quick look at the 1981 bestseller list for nonfiction books clearly reveals the primary concern of most Americans that year—money. Whether *Sylvia Porter's Money Book* or *How To Prosper During the Coming Bad Years* or *Crisis Investing*, the books that sold that year were those that claimed to tell people how they could make the most of their money in an age of rampant worldwide inflation.

The effects of double-digit inflation are all around us. At the gas pump we discover that the gallon of gasoline we paid $.39 for in 1970 costs us nearly a dollar more in the 1980s. The individual shopping in 1981 for a house in the San Francisco Bay Area learned that the average cost of a single-family dwelling was $110,000. One year of liberal arts education at Stanford University costs $10,000. Heating costs, food prices, the cost of medical services—all are skyrocketing and there seems to be no end in sight. At this point the world has still not produced an economist who fully understands the cause of inflation or its cure. But while everything seems to be getting so expensive, there is still something that is totally free—our dreams! It doesn't cost a dime to dream about an expensive sports car, a cruise on the Love Boat, or a career as an actress or a doctor. All we have to do is to sit back, close our eyes, and let our imaginations take us where they will. And as long as we are able to restrict ourselves to dreaming in places other than on the freeway or in an important board meeting, our dreams won't cost us a thing.

The Death of Dreaming

Yet in my conversations with people over the last few years I have noticed a disturbing trend. It appears that fewer and fewer people take the time to dream significant dreams. Part of the reason we seem to have quit dreaming is that we have resigned ourselves to a fatalistic philosophy. We can't do anything about inflation, about starvation, about the escalation in the nuclear arms race, or about any other matter of significance in our world, so why fool ourselves into thinking we can? Why dream about the way things might be, when it is obvious that they never will be that way?

We have resigned ourselves to failure. We have become convinced that we can't overcome the powers that be, and that it is impossible to change the way things are. Instead of trying to swim upstream, to dream and hope for a better life for ourselves and our world, we have resigned ourselves to floating along with the current.

While some of us have quit dreaming because failure seems inevitable, others of us have quit because we have been drugged by contentment. We are quite content with the job we have, the home we live in, and the people we associate with, so why bother dreaming about anything else?

Contentment, it is true, can be a virtue. It is a virtue to be able to be happy with whatever God has given us by way of talents, possessions, and physical characteristics. But to become so content with our state of being that we quit growing in our spiritual lives, that we quit trying to influence our world for the sake of Christ, that we quit seeking to experience more of what God has promised us—that is a calamity!

Until we become a mirror image of the character of Jesus

Christ, we should not be content with our spiritual maturity. Until the whole world bows at the feet of Jesus Christ and confesses Him as Lord, we should not be content with the impact we have made on our world.

Until we have experienced the reality of all that God has promised us in His Word, we should not be content with the experiences of His power and grace and love that we have already enjoyed. If we as God's people are to change our world to the degree that God has sent us to do, we cannot allow ourselves to be drugged by contentment.

There's More to Life!

Have you ever had the desire to be more than you are, to see more than you've seen, to do more than you've done? The early Christians felt that urge. They couldn't help but have it after listening to Jesus' promises:

- "For truly, I say to you, if you have faith as a mustard seed, you shall say to this mountain, 'Move from here to there,' and it shall move; and nothing shall be impossible to you" (Matt. 17:20).

- "Truly, truly, I say to you, he who believes in Me, the works that I do shall he do also; and greater works than these shall he do; because I go to the Father" (John 14:12).

Greater works than Jesus did? Didn't He heal the blind and lame, turn water into wine, feed over 5,000 men plus women and children with five loaves of bread and two small fish? Didn't Jesus even raise the dead? Didn't He provide for the forgiveness of all humankind by His death on the cross? Didn't He found a movement that would eventually enlist millions of individuals and endure throughout the rest of history?

Yes, Jesus did all that and more. And yes, Jesus did tell His disciples that they would be able to do even greater things than He did.

Why should we dream? Because none of us have yet experienced all that God desires for us, and until we reach heaven we never will. There is always something more that God has for us. Jesus promised that we could do even greater works than He did, and we all have a long way to go just to catch up with Him!

The Apostle Paul was a great dreamer. He had dreams of seeing the whole known world come to faith in Jesus Christ, and perhaps more than any other individual, he took a giant step in making that dream become a reality. In a benediction he penned in his letter to the Ephesian church, Paul described the fantastic power of God with these words:

> Now to Him who is able to do exceeding abundantly beyond all that we ask or think, according to the power that works within us, to Him be the glory in the church and in Christ Jesus to all generations forever and ever. Amen (3:20-21).

How great is God's power? Great enough to do far more than we can even dream of! Where is that power? At work in us!

Some of us have quit dreaming because it seems futile and pointless. We have resigned ourselves to fatalism and failure. But we have available to us the power to accomplish more than we can imagine even in our most outlandish dreams! Dreaming isn't futile. Trying to change our world is not a waste of time. It can be done, because God's unlimited power is at work in us. How do we unleash that power? We begin by dreaming big dreams.

Fortunately there are still many people who have the urge to be more than they are, to see more than they've seen, to do more than they've done. But along with that desire goes an inevitable frustration of not fulfilling your dreams. How frustrating to want so badly to excel, to reach your highest potential, and then to fail time after time. How frustrating to live in mediocrity when you ache to be the best.

God has created us to want and to seek fulfillment, to want and to pursue life in its abundance, to want and to quest for excellence. When instead of finding fulfillment, abundance, and excellence we experience only futility, emptiness, and a nauseous mediocrity, our frustration is intensified.

But there is a way out! Frustration is not final. With God's power and grace at work in your life, your frustration can become fulfillment! God can help you to make your dreams—of adventure, of being the best you can be, of life lived to the limit—come true.

Dream!

Fulfilling the desire to do, be, and experience more starts by dreaming. To dream is to visualize what you want to have happen in your life. While daydreaming comes naturally to most of us, constructive dreaming takes some hard thought and sometimes even a bit of research. It involves deciding what is really important to us.

What do you want out of life? What would you like to experience, to achieve, to be? To get your juices flowing here's a short list of possibilities:

- to become an outgoing, well-liked person
- to travel to Europe, Israel, Alaska, China, or Samoa
- to graduate from a highly respected university
- to become an accomplished musician or artist
- to become a successful business entrepreneur
- to build your own house
- to have a happy, successful marriage
- to be an outstanding mother and homemaker
- to become a widely read author
- to explore the solar system
- to discover a cure for cancer
- to climb a mountain few people have ever climbed
- to be a revolutionary for God
- to be an honest, effective politician

If you've never really thought about what you want to give to life and what you want to get out of it, now is the time. Ask yourself, "If I could do anything I wanted to do—no matter what the cost involved, education necessary, or time it would take—what would I really like to do?" The first step in making your dreams come true is to dream.

Dr. Lloyd John Ogilvie is the senior pastor of the 8,000-member First Presbyterian Church in Hollywood, California. In his commentary on Colossians, Dr. Ogilvie allows the reader a brief glimpse into his personal experience of the Christian life:

> The reason I lived for so long without realizing the power of the Holy Spirit is that I was attempting only those things which I could do easily on my own strength. One day a friend asked me what I was daring to do that only God's power could accomplish. I was alarmed to discover that my life was limited, cautious, and fearful.

What limited Dr. Ogilvie's life? His own small thinking, his unwillingness to stretch out and try something beyond his normal abilities. But Dr. Ogilvie continues:

> The adventure of Christianity began when I moved beyond self-reliance to dare to attempt those guided impossibilities that only the Lord could achieve (*Loved and Forgiven*, Regal, p. 23).

Sometimes we are afraid to dream big dreams because we don't want to seem self-centered or proud or as if we want to be better than other people. We don't want it to sound as if our goal is to be great, to be famous, to be a success. So we confine ourselves to small dreams and small goals, to very manageable and easily achievable tasks.

But that's not what God wants for us! God wants us to trust Him enough to dream of and then attempt some great, significant works! To limit ourselves to only those tasks or goals we know we can handle isn't humility but a lack of faith in the power of God.

When did the adventure of the Christian life, the life without limits, begin for Lloyd Ogilvie? When he began to dream about and dare to attempt those "guided impossibilities," that he knew could only be accomplished by the immeasureable power of God. The first step in making our dreams—God's dreams—for us come true is to creatively visualize what we most want.

Evaluate the Obstacles

After you've spent some time dreaming, choosing, and visualizing your goals, you need to take a second step. This step is so natural that it will take place whether you think about it or not. It is to evaluate the obstacles between where you are now and where you want to be.

Usually the first thought that comes to mind after we've chosen and visualized our goal is, "I'll never be able to do it because. . . ." We humans have the tendency to be very negative. The easiest thing in the world is to think of all the reasons why we can't do what we'd really like to do.

Just to help you speed up the process a bit, here's a list of possible obstacles that you might face in the pursuit of your dream:

- I'm too young
- I'm too old
- I'm physically handicapped
- I don't have the money
- I don't have the time
- I don't have the energy
- I'm not intelligent enough
- I'm not creative enough
- I'm too shy
- I'm not attractive
- I don't know the right people
- It's too hard to change at this stage in my life

Some of these are imposing hurdles. Some of them *may* be impossible for us to overcome with the matrix of gifts and resources God has given us. We all do have limitations, and there will be times when we will fail. Don Brenneman, the music minister at the church I belong to, and also a good friend, has made it clear to me that God has placed some very severe restrictions on my singing ability. But a failure isn't the person who doesn't reach his goal, who doesn't perform perfectly, or achieve all of his desires. A failure is the person who doesn't even try.

At a seminar given by Dr. Francis Schaeffer, I happened to read an article about a man named Craig Vick. My curiosity was aroused when I noticed that our first names were identical, our ages were the same, and that Craig is a preacher like I am. But Craig Vick can also do quite a number of things that I can't do. He is a tenor soloist. He is a champion chess player. He can repair televisions. He is a scuba diver and an artist. He has begun to do some writing as well as preaching. Craig Vick is a very gifted person.

It might also interest you to know that Craig Vick was born with only one leg and no arms below the elbows. For many of us, those handicaps would be enough to discourage us from even trying to live a normal life, from even attempting to paint or repair televisions or go to graduate school or write. We would more than understand if Craig Vick chose to just live out his life at home where he would be protected from the stares of strangers. But Craig Vick wouldn't settle for anything less than the best he could be. He dreamed some big dreams, and risked failing in order to make them become reality.

It is essential to make an honest assessment of your abilities and resources, to recognize what your obstacles may be. But obstacles and limitations are not roadblocks. They are not dead ends. Through the power of God your obstacles can become opportunities, your stumbling stones can become your stepping stones. Don't stop dreaming or trying because there is an obstacle in the way. Ask God to show you a way around it. Don't stop until God stops you.

Get Out of the Boat!

After you have chosen and visualized a goal and after you have honestly evaluated the obstacles in the light of the power of God, there remains but one step to take in order for your God-given dreams to become a reality. This is the hardest step of all, the place where more failures take place than at any other step of the way. The best person to illustrate this step is none other than that loveable leader of the Twelve himself, the Apostle Peter.

My favorite story involving Peter is the one in which Jesus walked on water.

Then Jesus made the disciples get into the boat and go ahead of Him to the other side of the lake, while He sent the people away. After sending the people away, He went up a hill by Himself to pray. When evening came, Jesus was there alone; by this time the boat was far out in the lake, tossed about by the waves, because the wind was blowing against it.

Between three and six o'clock in the morning Jesus came to the disciples, walking on the water. When they saw Him walking on the water, they were terrified, "It's a ghost!" they said, and screamed with fear.

Jesus spoke to them at once. "Courage!" He said. "It is I. Don't be afraid!"

Then Peter spoke up. "Lord, if it is really You, order me to come out on the water to You."

"Come!" answered Jesus. So Peter got out of the boat and started walking on the water to Jesus. But when he noticed the strong wind, he was afraid and started to sink down in the water. "Save me, Lord!" he cried.

At once Jesus reached out and grabbed hold of him and said, "What little faith you have! Why did you doubt?"

They both got back into the boat, and the wind died down. Then the disciples in the boat worshiped Jesus. "Truly You are the Son of God!" they exclaimed (Matt. 14:22-23, GNB).

Only two people in the New Testament walked on water. One was Jesus Christ, the Son of God, the Creator of the universe. We would expect it from Him. But who would ever imagine that the only other person to walk on water, for even a short time, would be Peter?

Have you ever asked yourself why Peter, of all people, was

able to walk on water? What distinguished Peter from the other disciples in the boat? What made him special?

It wasn't money. Matthew had come from a wealthier background than Peter. It wasn't intelligence. He was just a plain old fisherman. It wasn't political pull. Simon the Zealot had a great deal more influence politically than Peter.

The only thing to distinguish Peter from the other disciples is that he got out of the boat! How simple! It didn't require looks, talent, money, intelligence, or any other ability or resource. All it took was the willingness to take a chance, to risk. What's the moral of the story? If you want to walk on water, you have to get out of the boat!

After you have chosen and visualized your goal, and eva-luated your obstacles, the third step to take in making your dreams a reality is to get out of the boat, to take a chance and give it your best shot. To make your dreams a reality doesn't necessarily require beauty, bucks, brains or brawn. All it re-quires is the courage to take a risk, to get out of the boat and try walking.

Rowland Bingham had a dream of taking the message of the Gospel to the interior of Africa. At that time white men simply did not set foot on that soil. No mission board would accept him and no church would support him. So he hopped a freighter and worked his way to Egypt, finally reaching the interior of Africa after seven years of traveling.

Bingham spent the next seven years learning languages and sharing the Gospel of Christ as well as he could. But in all those years not one person was converted. Even so, Rowland Bingham continued. He had a dream and he wasn't ready to let go of it yet.

As a result of Rowland Bingham's work in the interior of Africa, thousands of Africans finally experienced the power and love of God. After those first 14 frustrating, fruitless years, Bingham had the thrill of seeing his dream come true. Today, the Sudan Interior Mission, devoted to continuing the work Bingham began, is one of the most successful missionary agencies in Africa. Why? Because one man was willing to get out of his boat and take a risk despite the obstacles that stood in his way.

I met Steven when he was a seventh-grader, just starting out in the world of junior high. Because I was going to be his counselor at camp for a week, I had been told a little about him, but was still unprepared to deal with what took place those first two days. Steven had been crippled by scoliosis, a curvature of the spine. His elbows were fused at an angle, his legs were as thin as my forearms, his nose and ears were too big for his face, and he could hear only with a hearing aid. Steven had the good fortune to have a family who loved him and let him know how special he was. But when he was away from his family, especially in a strange environment, Steven was scared to death. At camp he cried almost continuously for two days.

Finally, after those two days in which we held Steven's bony hands and prayed with him and let him know that he was special to us, Steven stopped crying. After wiping the tears from his large eyes, Steven took a deep breath and looked around. He noticed that there were some activities available at camp that he enjoyed. After a little coaxing we convinced Steven to go into the craft shop and pick out a project to work on. Steven became so engrossed in carving out a wood plaque that he hardly noticed when we slipped away to leave him awhile to fend for himself.

As the week wore on Steven became more and more trusting, gradually responded to the other kids when they asked questions or smiled at him. And as Steven opened himself up and came out of his shell, he was bombarded with love! The last night of camp was our talent and skit night. For Steven's talent he walked up the aisle holding the plaque he had made, with John 3:16 carved into it. When he reached the front, all of the kids and counselors stood up and wildly applauded the precious person that God had given us that week. The smile on Steven's face that night and his constant chattering through the rest of the evening were outstanding evidences that Steven was a changed person.

Steven had a very difficult time getting out of his boat. It was hard to leave the security of family and home and be thrust into the middle of 60 strangers. But when Steven forced himself to slide his scrawny toes out of the safety of his boat and dive into a new experience and new relationships, he discovered that the risk was more than worth it. By the end of the week Steven was walking on water!

Would you like to walk on water? Would you like to experience the joy of being loved, of being intimate, of being accepted? Would you like to break out of the old routine and invest your life in something significant? Would you like to be a part of changing our world? Do you have a desire to do more, to see more, to be more? If that is what you want, then you have to be willing to take a chance. You have to be willing to risk a broken heart, a broken ego, or even, like Jesus, a broken life. But God promises that the risks will always be worth it. If you want to walk on water, if you want to see your frustrations turned into fulfillment, you have to get out of the boat!